Michigan

MICHIGAN BY ROAD

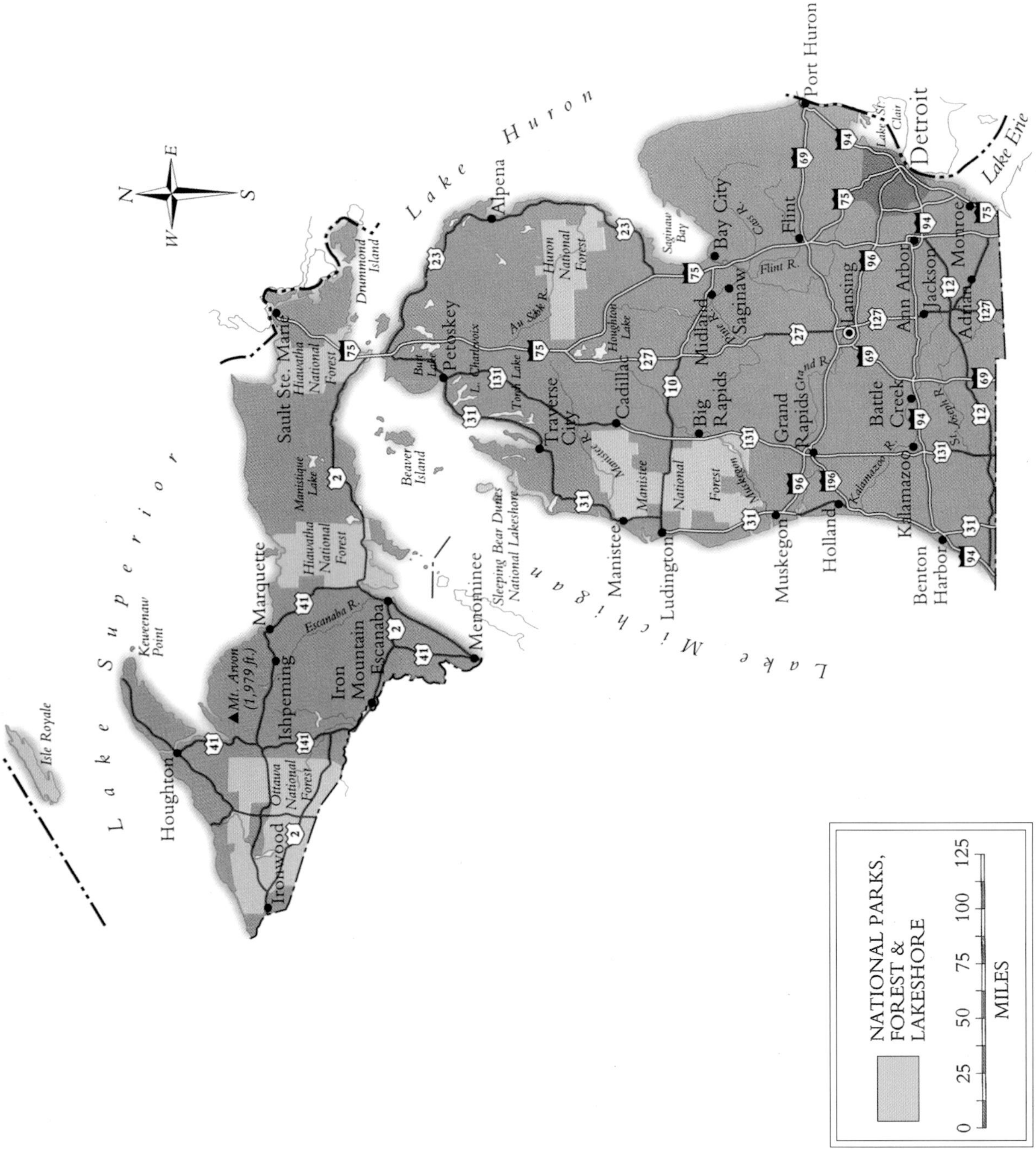
Lake Superior
Lake Huron
Lake Michigan
Lake Erie
Lake St. Clair
Isle Royale
Keweenaw Point
Houghton
Ironwood
Ottawa National Forest
Ishpeming
Mt. Arvon (1,979 ft.)
Iron Mountain
Escanaba
Escanaba R.
Marquette
Menominee
Hiawatha National Forest
Manistique Lake
Sault Ste. Marie
Drummond Island
Beaver Island
Sleeping Bear Dunes National Lakeshore
Petoskey
Burt Lake
L. Charlevoix
Torch Lake
Traverse City
Alpena
Huron National Forest
Au Sable R.
Houghton Lake
Cadillac
Manistee R.
Manistee
Manistee National Forest
Muskegon R.
Ludington
Big Rapids
Midland
Saginaw
Saginaw Bay
Bay City
Cass R.
Flint R.
Flint
Port Huron
Detroit
Lansing
Ann Arbor
Jackson
Monroe
Adrian
Grand Rapids
Grand R.
Muskegon
Holland
Kalamazoo R.
Kalamazoo
Battle Creek
St. Joseph R.
Benton Harbor
N
S
E
W
2
12
23
27
31
41
69
75
94
96
127
131
141
196
10
NATIONAL PARKS, FOREST & LAKESHORE
0
25
50
75
100
125
MILES

Celebrate the States

Michigan

Marlene Targ Brill

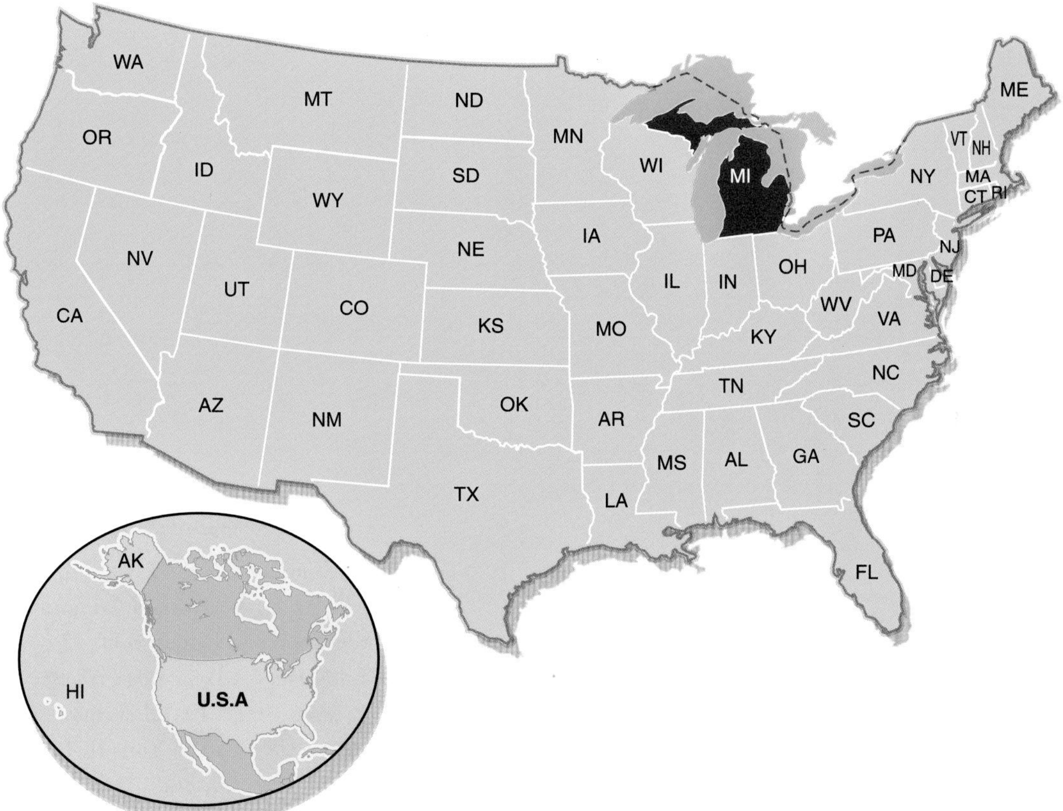
WA
MT
ND
MN
ME
OR
ID
WY
SD
WI
MI
NY
VT
NH
MA
CT
RI
IA
NV
UT
CO
NE
PA
NJ
OH
IL
IN
MD
DE
CA
KS
MO
WV
KY
VA
NC
TN
AZ
NM
OK
AR
SC
MS
AL
GA
TX
LA
FL
AK
HI
U.S.A

Marshall Cavendish Benchmark
New York

Marshall Cavendish Benchmark
99 White Plains Road
Tarrytown, NY 10591-9001
www.marshallcavendish.us

All Internet sites were correct and accurate at time of printing.

Library of Congress Cataloging-in-Publication Data
Brill, Marlene Targ.
Michigan / by Marlene Targ Brill.—2nd ed.
p. cm. — (Celebrate the states)
Summary: "Provides comprehensive information on the geography, history, wildlife, governmental structure, economy, cultural diversity, peoples, religion, and landmarks of Michigan"—Provided by publisher.
Includes bibliographical references and index.
ISBN-13: 978-0-7614-2351-5
ISBN-10: 0-7614-2351-6
1. Michigan—Juvenile literature. I. Title. II. Series.
F566.3.B75 2007
977.4—dc22
2006008181

Editor: Christine Florie
Editorial Director: Michelle Bisson
Art Director: Anahid Hamparian
Series Designer: Adam Mietlowski

Photo research by Connie Gardner

Cover Photo: Joe Sroka/Dembinsky Photo Associates

The photographs in this book are used by permission and courtesy of; *Corbis:* Lowell Georgia, 8, 91; W. Cody, 10; Joseph Sohm, 15, 72, 100; Layne Kennedy, 17; James L. Amos, 18; Richard Cummins, 28, 76, 96, 103; Medford Historical Society Collection, 44; Underwood and Underwood, 47; Bettmann, 50, 52, 130; Andrew Sacks, 54; Mark E. Gibson, 56; Ed Kashi, 62; Peter Yates, 67, 85; Steve Liss, 77; Ed Quinn, 84; Phil Schermeister, 93, 126; MacDuff Everton, 109, 110; Ed Wargin, 111; Tim Davis, 119; Ronald Wittek, 128; Reuters, 133; *Dembinsky Photo Associates:* Carl R. Sams II, 12, 22; Rod Planck, 14, 20; Jim Roetzel, 118; *Alamy:* Ed Reschke, 21; Jim West, 64, 86, 101; Dennis MacDonald, 124; *AP Photo:* Al Goldis, 74; *Getty:* Stephen Krasemann, 19; Hulton Archive, 45; David Hanson, 59; Richard H. Johnston, 89; Altrendo, 115 (top); Michael Melford, 123; *Photo Researchers:* James L. Amos, 24; *The Granger Collection:* 31, 37, 38; *North Wind Picture Archive:* 33, 35, 36, 41; *The Image Works:* Jim West, 65, 80, 82; Sonda Dawes, 69; Marilyn Genter, 115 (bottom); *SuperStock:* Richard Cummins, 97, 99; age footstock, 94,105; Tom Brakefield, back cover.

Printed in China
1 3 5 6 4 2

Contents

Michigan Is . . .

Michigan is a varied land . . .

". . . such an abundance of wild strawberries, raspberries and blackberries that they fairly perfumed the air of the whole coast with the fragrant scent of ripe fruit."

—Ottawa chief Andrew Blackbird

"We in Michigan are blessed because within the borders of our state are almost numberless places at which we can enjoy quiet seclusion, unmatched natural beauty, and escape from the daily grind."

—author and nature lover Tom Powers

. . . with creative people.

"I'm tough, ambitious, and I know exactly what I want. . . . A lot of people are afraid to say what they want. That's why they don't get what they want."

—pop singer Madonna

"Machines are to a mechanic what books are to a writer. He gets ideas from them, and if he has any brains, he applies those ideas."

—revolutionary automobile maker Henry Ford

Many fought for what is fair . . .

"We were used as utility pilots—towing targets for gunnery practice, delivering planes to squadrons—you name it, we did it."

—World War II military pilot Dorothy Eppstein

"We must recognize there are other disadvantaged people. . . . What we're talking about is [fostering] peaceful social change."

—union leader Walter Reuther

"For the freedom of my twenty-two million black brothers and sisters here in America, I do believe that I have fought the best that I knew how, and the best that I could, with the shortcomings that I have had."

—Black Revolution leader Malcolm X

. . . prospered among different people,

"I was lucky to grow up in Michigan, with its great cross-section of people. . . . The diversity of religions, race, and ethnic background exposed me to the world itself."

—President Gerald Ford

"How beautiful we are in our diversity, borne here and cradled by the earth."

—Beaver Island author Mary Blocksma

. . . and changed the world.

"People always say I didn't give up my seat because I was tired, but that isn't true . . . the only tired I was, was tired of giving in."

—The black woman who refused to move to the back of a bus, sparking the Montgomery Bus Boycott and the civil rights movement, Rosa Parks

Michigan is a land of contrasts. The state includes rolling farmland, giant factories, and tree-lined highways. It boasts lively college towns, old mining and lumber camps, and quiet villages. Native Americans and immigrants built each community, turning natural resources into goods that have made America proud. But Michiganders, people from Michigan, hide most of their treasures. They tuck them down back roads or behind closed doors on city streets. Once discovered, however, these places spring to life with colorful histories, interesting people, and many surprises. This is Michigan's story.

Chapter One

The Wolverine State

Billions of years ago, glaciers, or ice slabs, crept over North America. They inched along, pushing and scraping, at different periods of time, or ice ages. Four different ice ages ground rock piles into lowlands and swamps. They carved valleys and deep lake beds. Large sections of earth shifted from land to water and back again. Prehistoric plants and animals lived and died as the Earth changed.

The last glacier formed about ten thousand years ago. As the glacier retreated northward, ice sculpted a giant landmass that included the area that is now Michigan. The glacier left soil, sand, and gravel. The melting waters cut riverbeds and filled the lake with water.

Huge lake beds and two smaller peninsulas—landmasses with water on three sides—appeared. Sparkling waterfalls, thick forests filled with wildlife, and unusual rocks surrounded the lakes on the peninsulas. The glaciers left rich soil for fertile farmland in southern Michigan. To the north, they shaped hills and valleys. These became Michigan's natural wonders, and they attracted settlers and visitors to the state.

Munising Falls wash over sandstone rock cliffs dating back 500 million years in Pictured Rocks National Lakeshore.

A DIVIDED LAND

The clear blue Straits of Mackinac separated Michigan's two peninsulas, as it does now. Dozens of islands near Michigan's shores became part of the state as well. Each area delighted newcomers with a wealth of wild treasures. The varied beauty inspired future lawmakers to create the state motto: "If you seek a pleasant peninsula, look about you."

Today, the mitten-shaped Lower Peninsula points its rounded hand north toward Canada. Waterways to the northeast outline the "thumb." Indiana and Ohio run along the south rim of the Lower Peninsula. Wisconsin is the only state to border the Upper Peninsula, or UP, on its southwest side.

At 5 miles long, the Mackinac Bridge was the longest suspension bridge in the world when it opened in 1957. Although others are longer now, the Mackinac is still one of the world's longest suspension bridges.

Mackinac Bridge links the Upper and Lower peninsulas.

The bridge connects Michigan's two peninsulas. With two peninsulas and some two hundred nearby islands, Michigan seems spread out. But its land size of 58,110 square miles ranks twenty-second among the United States. Michigan extends 490 miles long and 240 miles wide at its farthest points. Add bordering Michigan waters to the land area, and Michigan becomes the tenth largest state in the nation.

Besides its neighboring states, Michigan connects with another country—Canada. Each day drivers rush across the Ambassador Bridge over the Detroit River between downtown Detroit and Windsor, Ontario, or hurry through the underwater Detroit-Windsor Tunnel. This crossing is the only place along the nation's border where Canada lies south of the United States.

MICHIGAMA

Michigan's main attractions have always included its waterways. Upon entering the Great Lakes, American explorer Henry Schoolcraft wrote, "He who, for the first time, lifts his eyes upon this expanse, is amazed and delighted at its magnitude."

As the glaciers melted, they left Michigan bounded by four of the five Great Lakes. Lake Huron lies to the east, Lake Erie to the southeast, Lake Superior to the north, and Lake Michigan to the west. The Great Lakes comprise the largest bodies of inland water in the world. They contain 20 percent of the world's freshwater. These waterways have affected ways of life in Michigan for centuries. Even the state name comes from the Ojibwe word *michigama*, meaning "great water."

Waves from the Great Lakes crash onto three-quarters of the state's border. Their sandy shores provide eighty-five harbors and countless beaches. Michigan beaches are longer than those of any state except Alaska. They create the largest freshwater sand dunes in the world.

Some say they are also the most beautiful. Sandy floors anchor forests in the Upper Peninsula. Farther south, wavy grasses cover many dunes next to Lake Michigan. Michigan's portion of Lake Erie displays cattail marshes sprinkled with lotus blossoms in the fall.

Michigan's Grand Sable Dunes extend 5 miles between the Sable River and Au Sable Point along Lake Superior.

At Sleeping Bear Dunes National Lakeshore in the Lower Peninsula, sand mounds reach 400 feet high. Ojibwe legend says that the largest dune represents a sleeping mother bear. "Dunes can originate from different sources," park interpreter Alan Wernette explained. "At Sleeping Bear, the sand came from glaciers. Black bits in the fine sand are iron, a mineral not found in this region. Glaciers brought the iron particles from ancient mountains north of the UP."

Sometimes, signs of life from long ago lie under the dunes. No one knows how fossils of three species of ocean-swimming whales wound up in Tecumseh, Flint, and Oscoda. Geologists believe they swam up prehistoric lakes that no longer exist. The whales became stranded in the shallow waters and died, leaving their skeletons buried in the sand. Other fossils have been discovered in Ann Arbor, Arkona, and Mesick.

LAND AND WATER

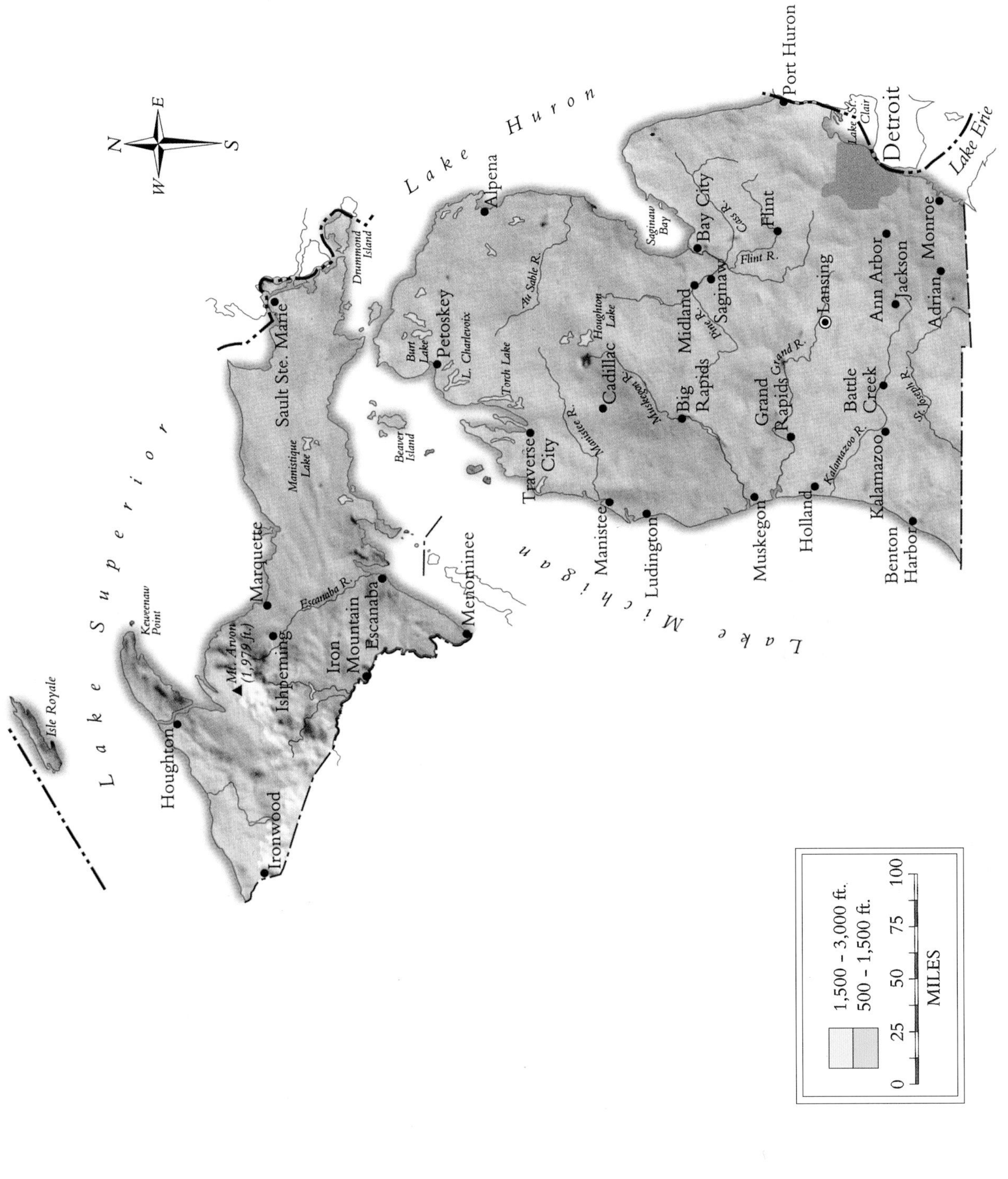

N
E
S
W
Lake Superior
Lake Huron
Lake Michigan
Lake Erie
Lake St. Clair
Isle Royale
Keweenaw Point
Mt. Arvon (1,979 ft.)
Houghton
Ironwood
Ishpeming
Marquette
Iron Mountain
Escanaba
Escanaba R.
Menominee
Manistique Lake
Sault Ste. Marie
Drummond Island
Beaver Island
Burt Lake
Petoskey
L. Charlevoix
Torch Lake
Traverse City
Au Sable R.
Alpena
Houghton Lake
Cadillac
Manistee R.
Muskegon R.
Manistee
Ludington
Big Rapids
Midland
Pine R.
Saginaw Bay
Bay City
Saginaw
Cass R.
Flint
Flint R.
Grand R.
Grand Rapids
Muskegon
Holland
Lansing
Kalamazoo R.
Kalamazoo
Battle Creek
St. Joseph R.
Benton Harbor
Jackson
Ann Arbor
Adrian
Monroe
Detroit
Port Huron
1,500 - 3,000 ft.
500 - 1,500 ft.
0
25
50
75
100
MILES

WATER WONDERLAND

Glaciers formed more than 11,000 inland lakes covering 40,000 square miles of Michigan. Countless streams, bogs, and marshes extend into forests and farmland. Michigan claims more freshwater than any other state. No wonder it became known as the Water Wonderland.

Central Michigan is home to Houghton Lake, the state's largest inland lake. Lake Gogebic is the largest lake in the Upper Peninsula. Three other important waterways—the Grand, Kalamazoo, and Saginaw rivers—flow into the Great Lakes from the heart of Lower Michigan. These water routes contributed to Michigan's role as a thriving logging state during the late 1800s.

Michigan's Boreal Forest is relatively flat from early glacial activity. Bogs, ponds, and lakes are therefore commonly found here.

Sands near the mouth of the Kalamazoo hide a famous Michigan ghost town called Singapore. The town was founded in the 1830s by New York land developers who hoped it would rival Chicago and Milwaukee as a lake port. By the 1870s, Singapore grew into a busy lumber town with three mills, two hotels, a bank, and many general stores. Once the lumber supply disappeared, the bustling waterfront harbor died. Folks moved north to livelier Saugatuck. Over time, Lake Michigan's shifting sands buried Singapore. Today, the town is remembered by a plaque overlooking Saugatuck Harbor.

The Upper Peninsula is waterfall country. More than 150 waterfalls plunge into the UP's many rivers and streams. The most famous is Tahquamenon Falls, which is 200 feet across and has a 50-foot drop.

The brown color of Tahquamenon Falls is not a result of muddy water. The color comes from a plant extract leached from cedar, hemlock, and spruce swamps upriver.

It is the second-largest waterfall in the United States east of the Mississippi River and where the second-greatest amount of water falls. Eastern poet Henry Wadsworth Longfellow was so taken with the falls, he wrote about it in his poem "The Song of Hiawatha."

FORESTS, ROCKS, AND ROLLING HILLS

Michigan's natural wonders attracted newcomers from around the world. Immigrants often found what they were looking for in Michigan—a place to remind them of home. Perhaps cold, forested northern hills recalled Finland, or flat Lower Michigan suggested Dutch tulip and celery fields.

Much of the 300-mile-long Upper Peninsula is forest. In Hartwick Pines State Park, north of Grayling, some trees stand 150 feet tall and are three hundred years old. Before logging, pine trees dominated the peninsula. In the mid-1800s, enough pines grew throughout Michigan to build a floor that would cover the entire state. The pines mingled with evergreen trees to blanket the northern region. Hardwood oak, maple, elm, ash, hickory, and basswood filled land farther south.

Within fifty years, however, the pine forests disappeared, along with other types of trees as well. In 1899 the state began to plant new trees. Many people still worried that the loss of trees would put an end to the lumber industry and increase soil erosion. In 1929 the federal Civilian Conservation Corps increased the number of trees planted. With these early successes came claims that Michigan was the first state with an eye toward conserving its natural resources.

Interest in preserving the environment continues to this day. Forests cover 53 percent of the state, and the forest product industry thrives. Now white birch, maple, and beech trees have replaced many pines. "In spots, trees are so thick sunlight never reaches the ground," one traveler noted.

Michigan's few mountains rise in the western Upper Peninsula. Here sandstone cliffs meet the shoreline. The highest point is Mount Arvon, at 1,979 feet. The area's many rock formations create a rugged wilderness.

Underground, the peninsula holds a wealth of minerals. Copper and iron triggered the nation's earliest mineral rushes. Iron mines still operate near Marquette. Limestone, oil, and gas fields contribute to the state's economy, while colorful agates, jasper, and greenstone thrill rock collectors.

At least 320 Michigan islands rise from the Great Lakes. Of these, Isle Royale in Lake Superior is the largest. The federal government obtained the 45-mile-long island along with the entire western Upper Peninsula from the Ojibwe in 1842. One reason was that the government wanted the Isle Royale copper mines. By 1900 the mines closed, leaving the island's natural harbors and interior lakes to nature lovers.

Lake Superior meets the sandstone cliffs at Grand Island.

The Lower Peninsula reveals many different faces. Michigan's major cities developed on the state's flatland. Beyond the larger towns lie unspoiled overlooks, sandy beaches, and rolling farmland.

Most of Michigan's farms are in the southern third of the mitten. Fruit orchards line the western portion of Interstate 94 and the Lake Michigan shoreline. Heading north, farms fade into forests, quaint harbors, and lakes. Steep banks climb to 300 feet on either coast.

Famous Illinois-born author Ernest Hemingway wrote some of his best lines at his home near Petoskey in northwestern Michigan. Images of wild game, leaping fish, and quiet lakes surrounded by woods appeared in many of his books. "The woods ran down to the lake and across the bay. It was beautiful in the spring and summer, the bay blue and bright and usually whitecaps on the lake out beyond the point," Hemingway wrote in *Up in Michigan*.

Crops, such as corn, beans, and blueberries grow on the more than 52,000 farms in Michigan.

ANIMALS, BIRDS, AND FISH

Thick Michigan forests hide white-tailed deer from black bears, coyotes, timber wolves, and an increasing number of sport hunters. Isle Royale is home to fewer than 500 moose. Packs of wolves feed on the animals, keeping the moose numbers down. Beavers, otters, raccoons, and foxes roam freely through the many state and federal parks and forests of both peninsulas. Some scour endless streams for trout, walleye, bass, perch, salmon, smelt, and northern pike. Others gnaw on acorns, mushrooms, and blueberries, which often outnumber wildflowers on the plains. Furbearing animals first lured fur traders to Michigan. Today, small-game hunting continues to draw visitors.

Tall pines and marshy shorelines help protect 350 bird species that pass through Michigan. Large populations of pheasant, wild turkey, partridge, quail, and grouse roam freely. The state was the first in the nation to establish a network of rest stops for migrating Canada geese. Controlled nature areas at Sturgeon River and Seney attract many geese, ducks, and trumpeter swans.

The wooded acres of Isle Royale are the perfect home for the red fox.

Ruffed grouse prefer forested land for their habitat.

Michigan is home to several controlled populations of elk, antler moose, and small gray wolves. The Michigan Natural Features Inventory Project track these and other endangered or threatened wildlife and their habitats statewide. Staff and volunteers monitor brush and forests for animals and birds, such as copperbelly water snakes and the threatened Canada lynx and red-shouldered hawk. Once the investigation is finished, staff recommend the best way to preserve wildlife habitats.

A similar project, the Michigan Clean Water Corps, uses volunteers from communities across the state to monitor water quality in the state's streams and lakes. The project includes two programs: one for lakes and one for streams. With the lake program, volunteers measure chemicals in their nearby lakes. The lake monitoring program began in the 1950s and is the second oldest in the nation. Volunteers for the stream program look for insects and habitats that may affect food and environments for fish.

This program began in the 1990s. Both programs have been used for local decision making about land use. Recently, the state expanded these programs to include trash cleanup along the banks of waterways.

One particular threat to waterways is the zebra mussel. These 1- to 2-inch striped-shell creatures originally came from the Caspian Sea between Europe and Asia. Zebra mussels attach themselves to hard surfaces, such as clams, industrial pipes, or boats, and travel easily. Once they reach a new waterway, zebra mussels quickly multiply, taking over freshwater habitats. One square yard of zebra mussels holds as many as 70,000 mussels. They clog water pipes and destroy areas where fish spawn. "They were first identified in Lake St. Claire [near Detroit] in 1988 and have spread like crazy," said Marcia Woodburn of the Great Lakes Basin Program. "They are now found in the Great Lakes and pockets of inland lakes."

Zebra mussels have become a nuisance by invading freshwater lakes and rivers. They clog pipes and deplete the food supply of freshwater fish.

Several programs work to reduce the threat of zebra mussels. Current studies explore the best way to rid waters of them. Many factories install specially coated pipes and other equipment to prevent mussels from attaching. This method costs companies millions of dollars. Some mussels are removed by mechanical scrapers, high-pressure spraying, or chemicals. So far, no one method has proved to be 100 percent effective, but research continues to find ways to rid waterways of this threat.

MANAGING DEER

Before Europeans settled in the state, large numbers of deer gathered among the Lower Peninsula's wetlands, bogs, and forests where food was plentiful. Then settlers and farmers cleared southern Michigan. By 1870 most deer had headed north, where they found food in the open spaces and brush left after logging. Within ten years, the northern herd had multiplied to about one million deer.

In 1885 lawmakers realized that something had to be done to control the number of deer—for the sake of the deer and the surrounding communities. For decades they passed laws to balance the needs of deer and humans. Some laws either shortened or lengthened deer hunting season, depending upon the nearby herd's size. Other laws limited the number of deer killed per hunt. Still, deer problems continued. During the 1930s, discussion centered on how to limit the number of deer hurt by cars and trucks. The following decades brought more housing complexes and new golf courses. Hungry animals roamed these developments looking for food.

Beginning with a 1971 law, a new policy began. For each deer hunting license sold, $1.50 of the cost went toward improving and maintaining deer habitats. This included buying land. The idea was to acquire land with enough food and shelter for healthy deer to live. Today, millions of dollars have been spent on improving habitats for deer. But Michiganders received the best payoff. More than 700,000 of the 3.8 million acres of state forests have been paid for by hunting license fees. These beautiful lands are open for the public to enjoy.

RAIN, SNOW, SHIPWRECKS

"In winter we ski, ice-fish, ice skate, and play hockey. In summer, we have tons of festivals," a proud Kalamazoo resident said. "You have four seasons here, which you don't get in California or the lower states."

For most Michiganders, different seasons mean year-round fun. Northern Michigan hosts an annual snowmobile festival in mid-March, which is late for snow season in most of the country. Up and down the Lake Michigan shoreline, harbor towns organize Venetian Night boat parades and water ski races in the summer.

The state's waterways soften the sometimes extreme climate, making winters less frigid and summers more pleasant. Large lakes tend to take the edge off bitter winter temperatures and cool the summer air because they are slow to heat and cool. This is what weather forecasters call the "lake effect." The results are gentle snowy winters, long growing seasons, and great fruit harvests in summer.

Inland, however, temperatures can swing to extreme highs and lows, depending upon where in the state they are reported. The highest recorded temperature is 112 degrees Fahrenheit on July 13, 1936, in Mio. The lowest temperature dipped to -51 degrees on February 9, 1934, at Vanderbilt. Average yearly rainfall between 30 and 38 inches varies by location within the state, also. The northern Upper Peninsula and southwestern Lower Peninsula receive the most rain.

Michigan is prone to severe storms. One of Grand Rapids' worst rainstorms occurred on July 26, 1883. Driving rains pelted the city for a record two weeks, raising the Grand River to dangerous levels. Lumberjacks floated their logs downstream in preparation for a flood. In their rush, they caused a 7-mile logjam above a railroad bridge. The jam broke suddenly, sending more than 600,000 logs crashing downriver.

Brave lumberjacks built boons that stopped the logs just short of Lake Michigan. No lives were lost, but property damage was heavy and the region's logging industry was shut down for years.

Violent storms over the Great Lakes have taken their toll on shipping. Blustery winds and giant waves have downed more than four thousand ships. The "Big Blow of 1913" sank nineteen ships and damaged at least another nineteen. Winds topped 90 miles per hour across Lake Huron, whipping waves 35 feet high. The storm was one of the deadliest to strike the Great Lakes.

A winter storm on Lake Superior kicks up powerful waves.

The waters of Lake Superior are the cruelest. Whitefish Point, where ships enter and leave the lake, earned the name "Graveyard of the Great Lakes" for its dangerous waters. The worst storm there to date came on November 10, 1975. The *Edmund Fitzgerald* sank 17 miles northwest of the point, drowning the entire crew. Popular singer Gordon Lightfoot remembered the storm in his song "The Wreck of the *Edmund Fitzgerald*." In 1995 the ship's bell was pulled from the lake. Today, the Great Lakes Shipwreck Historical Museum at the Whitefish Point Lighthouse displays the bell, a reminder of the brave sailors who lost their lives.

PRESERVING MICHIGAN'S TREASURES

Michiganders are proud of their state's natural riches. Between logging and mining, however, they discovered years ago how easily resources can disappear. That's why Michigan began to protect the environment more than a century ago.

"We haven't had the problems of other states," said Jim Dufresne, who works for the Michigan state parks department. "When mining threatened to flatten our dunes, we passed laws to prevent sand mines. We now plant more trees than we log. We test water and air regularly, especially where we still see problems from large factories."

Since the state replaced forests lost to logging and fires, thirty million trees a year have been planted on private, state, and federal land. Seedlings grow at state nurseries until they are two years old. Then they are shipped around the state in bundles of five hundred to a thousand. "The large variety of trees in parks came from the hodgepodge of red and white jack pine and white spruce planted since the program began," said Wendell Hoover, a park interpreter.

Mining companies do their part to restore the land. One northern Michigan iron mine has replaced an entire wetland that it had polluted with iron dust. Steel factories have installed dust collectors to catch chemicals that pollute the air. Water used for energy is recycled. Such efforts help provide cleaner air and water for wildlife and Michiganders alike.

Problems still develop from pollution that happened long ago. In 2005 toxic dust seeped into Lake Michigan and Bay Harbor resort and homes along beaches near Petoskey. The pollution came from an old cement manufacturing plant that had buried piles of poisonous dust. Thinking the area was safe, developers built on top of the waste. Now metals and black liquid flow from under the resort and into Lake Michigan. The water is so polluted that anyone who wades up to 50 feet into the lake risks scarring their skin forever from the bleachlike waste. Parks closed to keep children safe from waste in the soil. Cleanup has begun, but it will take years to complete. Engineers have recommended installing large pumps to redirect the seepage. They plan to place waterproof caps over the cement dust that lies under the resort's golf course. The state takes the Bay Harbor problem as a warning. Several Great Lakes tourist towns were once industrial sites.

Many Michiganders believe that the best way to protect the environment is through understanding. State workers have helped children's museums plan exciting hands-on displays that focus on improving the environment. "We also have major resource centers for environmental education throughout the state," Ron Nagel, a state parks employee, explained. "Each center focuses on a specific issue. At Maybury State Park near Detroit we run a living farm for people who don't know where milk comes from."

Educational projects often focus on specific natural resources. The Wetlands, Wildlife and You Too project helped students learn about wetlands and how to preserve them. Students studied twelve different wetland plants and previewed a video project. With the Sauk River Adopt-A-Stream Project, trained personnel encouraged school and community groups to adopt a portion of the Sauk River. They promoted public understanding of how pollution hurts river quality and worked to find groups to clean trash and litter twice a year.

Fifth- and sixth-grade students study and monitor characteristics of the Rouge River.

Fourth graders throughout Michigan explore their state parks through the Great Parks, Great History-L.A.P.'s (Learn from the past, Appreciate the present, and Preserve our outdoor heritage) programs. Students experience a range of activities led by workers from the Department of Natural Resources.

Michigan still has a long way to go to end pollution, but educating businesses, students, and families is a major step toward cleaning up the state's cities, streams, and air.

The Landing of Cadillac

Chapter Two

Michigan Then and Now

People first appeared in Michigan about 12,000 years ago. They roamed through the region searching for food along the lakeshores. Ancient hunters trapped mastodons in bogs. They crafted stone spear points to cut caribou and other huge animals that they hunted for food and hides. In between hunts, they gathered blueberries, cranberries, and nuts to eat.

About 3000 B.C.E., the people living along Lake Superior discovered copper. They dug copper mines in the hills of the Keweenaw Peninsula and on Isle Royale. Copper became valuable for making tools, jewelry, and fish-hooks. The Lake Superior people traded these goods to other groups in exchange for shells and hides. Ruins of prehistoric mines still remain on Isle Royale. They represent the oldest metal mining in North America.

Until about 500 C.E., the people of Michigan got their food by gathering, fishing, and hunting. Between 500 and 1650 C.E., farming developed. Women dug soil ridges to drain water and control weeds. Corn and red beans became the main foods of people from southern Michigan. The ancient wanderers settled on farms. They were the ancestors of Michigan's modern Native Americans.

A statue of Antoine de la Mothe Cadillac, founder of Detroit, marks the city's settlement.

THE PEACEFUL TRIBES

By the 1600s, an estimated 15,000 Native Americans lived in Michigan. About 12,000 roamed the southern Lower Peninsula. Three major tribes called the Three Fires established roots within Michigan borders. They were the Ojibwe (also called Chippewa), Ottawa, and Potawatomi. Although many differences existed among them, the three tribes spoke the same language and shared similar cultural traits and overlapping territory.

As the earliest of the Michigan tribes, the Ojibwe were known as the Elder Brothers, or Keepers of the Faith. They lived mainly in the eastern portion of the Lower Peninsula and much of the Upper Peninsula away from Lake Michigan. The Ojibwe were mainly nomads. They moved their villages along the Great Lakes and inland waterways to find fish or game. They were expert boaters and trappers of small and large game, such as moose, deer, and caribou.

The Ottawa people, or Keepers of the Trade, occupied the western Lower Peninsula and the upper reaches of the Great Lakes. Like the Ojibwe, the Ottawa wandered the land around the Great Lakes in search of wild rice, animals, and berries. They caught fish in woven nets while sailing the Great Lakes.

The Potawatomi, or Keepers of the Sacred Fire, settled to the south, especially in areas around the Kalamazoo and Saint Joseph rivers and in neighboring Indiana. Unlike the other two tribes, the Potawatomi stayed in one place and farmed. They lived in dome-shaped huts made of bark and saplings. They built rectangle-shaped longhouses and sweat lodges for their ceremonies. For food, they grew corn, beans, and squash. They traded these foods with newly arrived settlers.

Ojibwe Indians are known for their birch bark canoes.

Other nations, such as the Menominee and Wyandot, lived peacefully among the tribes of the Three Fires. Beginning in the 1600s, however, Europeans built colonies along the Atlantic coast. Settlers forced the Iroquois from their hunting grounds in the Northeast. Homeless bands of Iroquois swept through parts of Michigan. They battled with the Ottawa. Some Iroquois drove the Wyandot into the Detroit region, where they attacked the Potawatomi and later the Ojibwe. The calm among Michigan native tribes ended forever.

THE FIRST FIREFLY: AN OJIBWE LEGEND

Nana-boo-shoo and Mu-kaw-gee hunted for food in the early days of Mother Earth. "Please fill our stomachs with food and spirit," they begged the first trout they saw from the water's edge. The trout agreed to be eaten. He had always wondered about the world without water. Now his spirit could find out what is was like first-hand as part of these creatures.

The Ojibwe hunters thanked the trout and the Great Spirit of water. Then they gathered wood for a cooking fire. As the fish baked, wonderful smells filled the forest. A hungry fly noticed and followed the smell to the fire. The fly darted among the flames, trying to reach the cooking fish. "Move away from the hot fire," warned Nana-boo-shoo. "We will share when the fish is done."

The fly was too hungry and impatient to wait. He dove at the fish again and again, hoping to snatch a bit. Each time, the heat proved too much. The angry fly buzzed louder and louder.

Nana-boo-shoo grew tired of the noisy fly and began to wave it away. By accident, he hit the fly, dashing it into the fire. The fly shot out of the flames, stinging and hot. To cool his burned tail hairs, he dive-bombed into the creek. When his tail no longer stung, the fly lifted it out of the water. Everyone gasped in surprise, including the fly. His tail blinked on and off. But the fly was thrilled just to be alive. From then on, he became a night insect, lighting the sky for Mother Earth each summer.

FRENCH TRADERS AND MISSIONARIES

The first Europeans to reach Michigan came by accident. The French had claimed land along the Saint Lawrence River in 1604. But they insisted that another waterway led to the Pacific Ocean and beyond to China. French adventurer Etienne Brulé traveled the Great Lakes in 1620 in search of that route. He landed near an Ojibwe fishing camp at Sault Sainte Marie, becoming the first known European to set foot in Michigan.

In 1634 another Frenchman, Jean Nicolet, followed the Great Lakes through the present-day Straits of Mackinac to Green Bay, Wisconsin. Nicolet was sure that his ship had reached China. He fired pistols to announce his arrival and dressed in colorful silks to greet China's leaders. Neither Nicolet nor Brulé ever reached Asia, but their stories of Michigan's unlimited furs and copper brought other adventurers.

French priests followed the explorers to preach Christianity to the local tribes. By 1660 a mission had been built at Keweenaw Bay. Eight years later, Father Jacques Marquette established the first permanent French settlement in Michigan at Sault Sainte Marie. Father Claude Dablon reported that the site was the perfect place for a mission, "since it is the great resort of most of the Savages of these regions, and lies in . . . route of all . . . French settlements."

A Jesuit missionary teaches Christianity to a Native American.

Native Americans welcomed the early traders. They eagerly exchanged soft beaver, mink, and fox furs for European trinkets. They taught French traders to speak native languages and to track animals through the network of Indian trails. The Ottawa showed traders how to construct their birch bark canoes and travel Michigan's streams, lakes, and rivers.

More traders arrived to build timber forts near large Native American settlements around Saginaw Bay and the Straits of Michilimackinac. In 1671 France constructed the first fort at Saint Ignace as a mission, Michilimackinac, which was later shortened to Mackinac. Within twenty years, the fort mushroomed into North America's busiest fur-trading center.

The fort's new commander envisioned something bolder. Antoine de la Mothe Cadillac asked the French king, Louis XIV, to build a large colony at the *place du détroit,* or the "place of the strait." The king agreed. On July 24, 1701, Cadillac sailed down the Saint Clair River to the Detroit River with fifty soldiers, fifty traders and craftspeople, and two priests. There they built Fort Ponchartrain from logs and dirt. Cadillac and his chief lieutenant sent for their wives, who became the first European women to live in Michigan. Ottawa, Huron, Ojibwe, and Miami villages moved near the fort. Soon Fort Ponchartrain flowered into a lively settlement to rival the fort at Saint Ignace. Cadillac's wilderness village eventually became the city of Detroit, the future industrial giant.

After Cadillac's success, France expanded its settlements in Michigan. To encourage emigration, the king offered anyone relocating to Detroit in 1748 a cow, a pig, a wagon, a patch of land, and some farm tools. Farms sprouted on the west bank of the Detroit River. Fifty families moved farther west to Fort Saint Joseph near the Kankakee River to plant fruit. "The finest vines, the richest district in all that country," one settler wrote.

Antoine de la Mothe Cadillac lands July 24, 1701, founding the colony that later became Detroit.

WINDS OF CHANGE

Fur trading threatened the Native American way of life. As Indian hunters sought more furs to trade for European goods, many gave up farming and took to the woods to hunt and trap. Increasingly, Indians depended on European traders for their daily needs. Meanwhile, many Europeans now settled in the area for good, rather than trading with the Indians and leaving.

As more French and British traders arrived, they competed for the Indian fur trade. From 1754 until 1760, the two nations fought a war for control of North America. Some Indians sided with the French while others fought with the British. The conflict became known as the French and Indian War. In the end, France suffered a horrible defeat.

After a century of settlement, the only signs of the French to remain in the area were the names on old forts and settlements.

Many Native Americans throughout the Midwest refused to accept British rule. The British treated the Indians poorly. British traders ended the long-standing French custom of exchanging gifts, such as much-needed tobacco, guns, food, and gunpowder, to show friendship. British governor Jeffrey Amherst wrote, "I cannot think it necessary to give them any presents by way of Bribes, for if they [the Indians] do not behave properly they are to be punished."

In Michigan, an Ottawa chief named Pontiac challenged other tribes to resist British and European customs. Warriors swept through Michigan in what became known as Pontiac's War. Forts at Saint Joseph, Sault Sainte Marie, and Michilimackinac fell within two weeks. Pontiac's warriors stopped at the well-guarded Detroit fort and surrounded it for five months.

Chief Pontiac urges tribes in the Great Lakes region to organize and fight against the British.

Unable to muster enough men to storm the stockade, Pontiac's warriors slowly scattered to find food. Pontiac left disheartened. Although minor outbreaks continued until 1796, Pontiac's War was the last major Indian revolt in Michigan.

THE ROAD TO STATEHOOD

The British managed to reclaim the forts, but they continued to fight—this time against American colonists. In 1775 colonists declared themselves free of British rule, launching the American Revolution (1775–1783). Although the war raged mostly in the East, the English moved Fort Michilimackinac to an island in the Straits of Mackinac to protect its supplies.

The new U.S. government created the territory of Michigan in 1805 with Detroit as its capital. When Lewis Cass became territorial governor in 1813, the population barely reached nine thousand and seemed unlikely to increase. Overgrown Indian trails hindered wagon travel.

Part of the plan for the territory involved a full-scale effort to control Michigan's Native Americans. In 1823 the first missionary school opened on Mackinac Island. Native children who lived at the school were taught to ignore their tribal customs and learn European ways. This first school averaged 150 students a year until it closed in 1837.

Lewis Cass was Michigan's second territorial governor. He led Michigan to statehood and founded the Historical Society of Michigan in 1828.

Government Indian schools eventually replaced those run by missionaries. But the message to the confused and lonely children was the same: Indian language, food, and dress were bad and European culture was good.

With Michigan's Native Americans under control, Cass launched a program to bring more European settlers to Michigan. Detroit, Ann Arbor, Monroe, and Pontiac newspapers published reports about Michigan's rich resources. New trails were cleared. Within five years, five passable trails extended from Detroit across the state.

The opening of New York's Erie Canal in 1825 offered the greatest new transportation link. Now East Coast ships could reach Michigan entirely by water. Detroit ships brought wheat, flour, whiskey, and a new product—lumber—to eastern markets. They returned with craftspeople and laborers to work on the Detroit docks.

Detroit's economy thrived as products were imported and exported to eastern markets by ship.

Immigrants soon discovered the Lower Peninsula's fertile rolling hills to the west. The federal government sold land at a bargain rate of $1.25 an acre. Eager pioneers cleared trees for farms. These first farms grew into the cities of Kalamazoo, Lansing, Battle Creek, and Jackson in the state's agricultural heartland.

Greed for pelts soon killed most of Michigan's animals and, with them, the fur trade. The state's Native Americans lost their livelihood. Many of the region's European traders turned to logging and farming. These new occupations required large amounts of land, which Europeans hoped to obtain by bargaining with Native Americans. "The land is ours," a Kalamazoo Indian told newcomers. "You have no right to hack the trees. Your chiefs are bad."

As early as 1736, pioneers had begun chipping away at Native American land. In the end, the Indians lost thirteen million acres of hunting ground and farmland. Some bands were expected to move west of the Mississippi River. Most stayed, only to be forced onto reservation land thirty years later. Life grew difficult for most Native Americans. Many people on reservations near Saginaw Bay, Grand Traverse, and the Upper Peninsula experienced hardships. Still, they fought to maintain their way of life.

SETTING STATE BORDERS

By 1832 Michigan had 86,000 people, enough to apply for statehood. But a serious problem existed between Michigan and the state of Ohio that kept them from becoming states. Both claimed the same 75-mile-long stretch of land along the southern rim of Michigan known as the Toledo Strip. After years of arguing, lawmakers drafted a compromise that gave Ohio the Toledo Strip. In exchange, Michigan received the western section of the Upper Peninsula, clearing the way for statehood. On January 26, 1837, Michigan became the twenty-sixth state to join the Union.

At first, Michiganders found the bargain insulting. The wild backwoods was a poor trade for a port at Toledo. Then geologists discovered large deposits of copper, iron, and limestone in the Upper Peninsula. Cities in the Lower Peninsula looked north for lumber to replace the dwindling fur trade. Hopes ran high that the Upper Peninsula could help Michigan prosper. French statesman Alexis de Tocqueville visited the north in 1831 and wrote, "In a few years these impenetrable forests will have fallen; the sons of civilization and industry will break the silence of the Saginaw."

Tocqueville's vision came true. By the mid-1800s, Michigan led the nation in copper and iron mining and lumber production. Wages of twenty to thirty dollars a month attracted loggers from Finland to the Upper Peninsula. Prospectors and miners flocked from Scotland, Ireland, and Sweden looking for riches. Lumber and mining towns appeared overnight. Farther south and west, towns expanded with sawmills and furniture factories made from these raw materials.

In 1847 the state capital moved to Lansing because it was a more central location. Lansing and other boomtowns created a demand for railroads to transport immigrants and goods. Railroad owners recruited workers from Germany, England, France, and Austria to clear land and lay tracks.

Congress allotted money to build a canal at Sault Sainte Marie. The Saint Marys River linked the Great Lakes and Lake Superior. But the 21-foot waterfall drop from Lake Superior to the lakes below posed a danger for ships. A lock on Canada's side had been destroyed in the War of 1812. In 1855 the United States acted to boost water travel. The Soo Locks, also known as Saint Marys Falls Canal, helped ships drop the 21 feet from Lake Superior into Lake Huron. Statesman Henry Clay told Congress in 1855 that the Soo Locks proved "a work beyond the remotest settlement of the United States, if not the moon."

During the mid-1800s, the logging industry prospered. Loggers from Europe came to the Upper Peninsula seeking work and good pay.

"MICHIGANIA"

In 1916 George Newman Fuller wrote in *Economic and Social Beginnings of Michigan:* "It was exceptional for a settler to emigrate directly from his place of birth to Michigan. He was much more likely to have a number of . . . stopping places; for example, he might be born in England, migrate with his parents to Connecticut, be educated in Vermont, engage in business in New York, and then spend some years on the frontier in Ohio . . . before finally settling in Michigan." This song traces just such a journey.

D
Come all ye Yan - kee farm - er boys, who would like to change your
Em
lot; With spunk e - nough to tra-vel be-yond your na - tive
A7 D G
spot; And leave be-hind the vil-lage where pa and ma do
D A7 D F♯m Bm7 Gm6 D A7 D
stay: Come go with me and set - tle in Mi - chi-gan - i - a.

For there's your Penobscot way down in parts of Maine,
Where timber grows in plenty but not a bit of grain.
And there is your Quaddy and your Piscataqua,
But these can't hold a candle to Michigania.

And there's the state of Vermont, but what a place is that?
To be sure the girls are pretty and the cattle very fat.
But who among her mountains and clouds of snow could stay,
While he can buy a section in Michigania.

And there is Massachusetts, once good enough, be sure,
But now she is always lying in taxation and manure.
She'll cause a peck of trouble but deal a peck will pay,
While all is scripture measure in Michigania.

And there's the state of New York, the people's very rich;
Among themselves and others have dug a mighty ditch
Which renders it more easy for us to find the way,
And sail upon the water of Michigania.

What country ever grew up so great in little time,
Just popping from a nursery right into life its prime?
When Uncle Sam did wean her, 'twas but the other day,
And now she's quite a lady, this Michigania.

And if you want to go to a place called Wastenaw,
You'll first upon the Huron; such land you never saw,
Where ships come to Ann Arbor right through a pleasant bay,
And touch at Ypsilanti in Michigania.

And if you want to travel a little farther on,
I guess you'll touch Saint Joseph where everybody's gone,
Where everything like Jack's bean grows monstrous fast, they say,
And beats the rest all hollow in Michigania.

Come all ye Yankee farmer boys with metal hearts like me,
And elbow grease in plenty to bow the forest tree,
Come, buy a quarter section, and I'll be bound you'll say,
This country takes the rag off, this Michigania.

CIVIL WAR

At the time Michigan became a state, Americans were debating over the right to own slaves. Michigan entered the Union as an antislavery state, and many Michiganders played important roles in freeing slaves. Detroit, Adrian, and Battle Creek became key strongholds of Michigan's Underground Railroad, the secret route to freedom in Canada for runaway slaves. Adrian's Laura Haviland hid so many runaways that she became known as Superintendent of the Underground.

The Civil War raged between 1861 and 1865 mainly to decide the slavery issue. Despite their own hardships, 145 Native American sharpshooters enlisted in Michigan's Company K. Of the 90,000 Michigan men (and one known woman posing as a man) who served, 14,000 died. Brave Michiganders captured Confederate president Jefferson Davis. They were the first western regiment to reach the nation's capital while it was under attack. After Michigan volunteers responded to his call for troops, President Abraham Lincoln declared, "Thank God for Michigan."

Men from Michigan enlisted as Union soldiers during the Civil War. These soldiers were from Michigan's 4th Infantry Regiment.

FIGHTING FOR FREEDOM

Sojourner Truth, a former slave, settled in Battle Creek during the 1850s. Truth traveled the country speaking to groups about rights for women and blacks, something few women or blacks were brave enough to do at the time. When the Civil War broke out in 1861, Truth wrote a song to the tune of "John Brown's Body" called "The Valiant Soldiers." She inspired the First Michigan Colored Regiment of 1,673 black soldiers marching out of Detroit with this moving stanza:

Look there above the center, where the flag is waving bright;
We are going out of slavery, we are bound for freedom's light;
We mean to show Jeff Davis how the Africans can fight,
As we go marching on.

HORSELESS CARRIAGES FOR THE WORLD

The Civil War created great demand for Michigan's natural resources. Wartime industries helped turn the state's trees and minerals into weapons and vehicles. Rapid development continued after peace was restored. Inventive businesspeople took Michigan's raw materials and built international companies that produced steel, ships, iron stoves, chemicals, and medicines. Mines and factories competed for workers to fill jobs in these and countless other businesses.

New products exported from the state thrust Michigan into the industrial spotlight. About one hundred railroad freight cars left Detroit factories each day. Shipbuilding in Bay City, Grand Haven, and Detroit flourished. Wagons built in Flint and carriages and horse-drawn streetcars from Detroit and Grand Rapids were known throughout the Midwest.

But the vehicles that caught the world's eye were the ones run by engine rather than horse—automobiles. Several people designed automobiles during the late 1800s, but it was Michiganders who put the world on wheels—and just in time. Logging had almost cleared the state's forests, and the economy seemed primed for a downturn.

Ransom Eli Olds and Frank Clark of Lansing opened Olds Motor Vehicle Company in 1897, the first company in the United States to mass produce gasoline-powered automobiles. The men constructed four automobiles their first year, which the public thought would never sell. Unshaken, Olds continued to improve the line until he manufactured more than five thousand automobiles by 1904. Olds's factory was the first to build automobiles in large numbers. But they were too expensive for most families.

Henry Ford, a mechanic from the Detroit suburb of Dearborn, experimented with different ways to create automobiles that the average family would be able to afford. After considerable study, he hired workers who

Henry Ford exhibits his first car in Detroit.

each handled one task of assembling the car. This assembly line system speeded construction, thereby reducing costs. In 1908 Ford's Model T sold for $950, which was $200 below the average price of a car. Within five years, Ford added a new plant in suburban Highland Park to assemble 200,000 vehicles a year. Each cost $550, a record low. By 1927 they cost only $290.

Carriage-builder William Durant added to the growth of Michigan's motor industry. Beginning in 1908, he cleverly bought up and combined several smaller automobile companies, including Olds, Buick, and Chevrolet. His giant General Motors Company rivaled Ford. Detroit blossomed into the center of the automobile industry, and factory towns, such as Pontiac, Saginaw, Lansing, and Flint, boomed. Hundreds of thousands of inexpensive gas-powered automobiles rolled off Michigan assembly lines bound for national and international markets. Detroit became the "Motor Capital of the World."

POPULATION GROWTH (1830–2000)

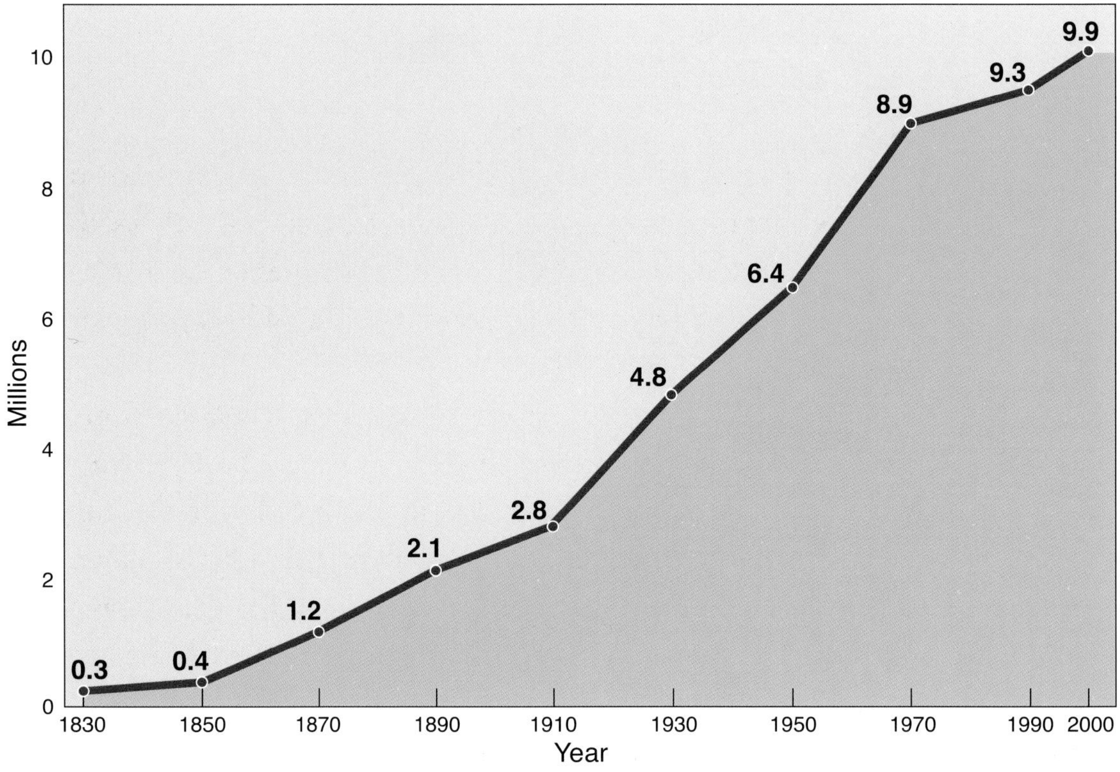
Millions
0
2
4
6
8
10
0.3
0.4
1.2
2.1
2.8
4.8
6.4
8.9
9.3
9.9
1830
1850
1870
1890
1910
1930
1950
1970
1990
2000
Year

WHEELS OF CHANGE

Cars greatly altered the way Michiganders lived. Automobile factories needed large supplies of iron, steel, copper, leather, rubber, oil, and gasoline. Michigan mines and factories worked overtime, often competing for laborers. Newcomers from Poland, Greece, Italy, Hungary, and Mexico mixed with earlier immigrants on assembly lines. Cars contributed to the beginning of suburbs, as roads and highways fanned out from major Michigan cities. By 1920 the state's population soared to 3.7 million people.

The population gradually shifted from farms to cities. Factory jobs promised fortunes unheard of from plowing fields. Fewer farmers were needed once tractors and other machinery replaced horse-driven plows. In 1920 only one-third of the population lived on farms, compared with two-thirds forty years earlier.

WORKER UNREST

The auto industry's success deeply divided Michigan's rich and poor. Auto company executives lived in luxury and wielded extreme power in local, state, and federal government. In 1953 General Motors president Charles Wilson boasted to the U.S. Senate, ". . . for years I thought 'What's good for General Motors is good for the country.' "

Industry profits often came at the expense of workers, however. Many were overcharged for tools, food, and housing provided by the company. Most suffered long shifts under filthy, unsafe conditions. Bosses speeded the machines to get more work from employees, creating greater danger. When wages increased at his plant to five dollars a day, double what most autoworkers earned, a Ford manager said: "Top management called us in and said that since workers were getting twice the wages, they wanted twice the work. . . . We simply turned up the speed of the lines."

Workers organized into unions, but auto company bosses refused to talk with union leaders. In December 1936 discontent came to a head at General Motors' Flint plant. The boss had fired several union men and now made plans to move equipment to a nonunion plant. Workers locked themselves in the factory for a sit-down strike. "The strike has been coming for a year," a striker wrote in his diary. "Speedup systems, favored workers, over-bearing foremen. You can go just so far you know, even with a working man."

Sit-down strikes spread to nearly sixty plants in fourteen states, leaving 150,000 workers idle. Genora Dollinger, a striker's wife, appealed to Flint women: "Come down here and stand with your fathers, brothers, husbands, and sweethearts. They're firing at unarmed men." The women marched with signs and sang until the strike ended. After forty-four days, General Motors finally met with union representatives. The motor company granted union

The members of the United Auto Workers union staged the first sit-down strike in Flint, Michigan in 1936.

bargaining rights to seventeen General Motors plants that were closed by sit-downs. Flint car-related factories became leaders in the recently formed United Automobile Workers (UAW), which grew into one of the most powerful unions in the world.

MODERN MICHIGAN

Union leaders bargained for raises, shorter workdays, fairer treatment, and safer conditions. Yet, for years after the UAW formed, few African Americans benefited from these contracts. Many Southern blacks had come north after World War I looking for factory jobs. What they found were the lowest-paying jobs under the worst conditions. Some automakers refused to hire African Americans or hired them only as janitors. Henry Ford assigned blacks to the foundry—the dirtiest, most dangerous, and most tiring work. Blacks distrusted the white-run unions and refused to join.

Detroit housing was terrible as well. Former mayor Coleman Young remembered how whites refused to rent or sell to blacks. "The result was overcrowding in the East Side Colored District, as it was called. . . . Housing was poor quality [yet] rents were two or three times as high as in white districts."

On a hot June 20, 1943, tensions erupted at Belle Isle Park near Detroit. Both races usually enjoyed the park, keeping their distance from each other. That day, a fight started between a white man and black man. Onlookers joined the brawl. Soon racial violence spread beyond the park. For two days, beatings, riots, and looting flared until the National Guard was called. When the disorder ended, nine whites and twenty-five blacks were dead and thousands of dollars in property lost. The riots unleashed a rage in blacks that lingered for years.

In July 1967, terrible race riots broke out in many parts of the nation, including Michigan. Downtown Detroit suffered huge losses from looted shops and burned buildings. Rioters leveled entire blocks. Roving gangs clashed with police and seven thousand National Guardsmen for five days. In the end, forty-three people died and the damage cost nearly $50 million. "This was a revolt of the underprivileged, overcrowded, hot and irritable who were fed up . . . and finally had a chance to be takers," Young said. This time, whites fled to the suburbs.

The 1970s brought troubled times for the automobile state. Gas shortages and serious competition from foreign carmakers threatened the country's auto producers for the first time. Michigan's unemployment skyrocketed as factories closed or reduced their workforces.

BARGAIN
TV SERVICE
LEETRONICS
RECORD PANACEA
898-4711
STEREO SERVICE
COLOR TV SERVICE

Detroit storefronts remained abandoned and boarded up in 1970, almost three years after the race riots.

Many companies moved factories to states with lower taxes and weaker unions, so they could pay their employees less.

Single-industry towns, like Flint and Saginaw, suffered most. People who were out of work found little money to buy goods. Stores closed and downtowns became eyesores with boarded-up storefronts. Detroit, the nation's sixth-largest city during the 1980s, had blocks of deserted buildings.

NEW CENTURY BLUES

Inner-city poverty and unemployment continued into the 1990s. Meanwhile, local and state governments scrambled to attract new businesses while keeping the old. Towns opened museums, restored neighborhoods, and built nature centers to attract tourists. By the end of the 1990s, Michigan's economic fortunes improved slightly.

After 2000, however, prospects reversed again. Gas prices spiked, as they did everywhere in the United States. The rise in fuel costs strained auto sales of big vehicles with poor mileage. The Iraq War took its toll on federal spending for states and soldiers who enlisted from Michigan. The biggest blow came after Ford and General Motors, the two largest automakers, announced several plant closings. Hundreds of thousands of jobs went overseas, where manufacturers could make their products cheaper and without unions making demands on behalf of workers. Unemployment soared, housing sales dropped, and crime increased. Detroit ranked second in the nation as the least safe big city.

Michigan has had severe setbacks, but it's not down yet. Natural resources are plentiful. Governor Jennifer Granholm hopes to create jobs in industries other than automobiles. Moreover, Michigan is a state with spirit, a fighting spirit that recalls the word *Tuebor* on the state flag, which is Latin for "I will defend."

Looney Tunes

Chapter Three

Great Lakes People

Michiganders come from a melting pot of cultures. But these varied groups tend to divide into pockets. Peninsulas, islands, and surrounding waterways have separated communities. "My community is different," said Anne Walker, a college student raised in Ann Arbor. "In Ann Arbor different races and religions live and go to school together. People from other Michigan towns who went to college with me had never met someone who was Jewish or black before. I loved growing up in such a cosmopolitan city and being exposed to a variety of people."

POPULATION SHIFTS

During the 1980s, Michiganders left the state in droves to find jobs. Young people from the Upper Peninsula migrated south or out-of-state looking for work. By 1995 population numbers reversed. For the first time in ten years, Michigan's population grew faster than that of most other states. Towns of fewer than 2,500 people grew at twice the rate of most U.S. big cities.

Resort areas in the northwest and western Lower Peninsula accounted for many of the population increases. "People moving north are older adults

Michigan hopes to keep younger residents within the state by reviving its cities and creating jobs and opportunities.

who want to retire in these beautiful areas," said Trina Williams, formerly of the state demographer's office. "People with summer homes here and in the west have decided to stay year-round. I guess everyone likes the slower pace."

After years of growth, the situation may change again. The 7.6 percent projected annual growth rate for Michigan pales compared with 29 percent for the nation. Experts agree that folks over sixty-five will continue to find the state attractive. But younger residents may look elsewhere, if many more companies close factories and cut jobs.

Seniors have remained in the state during their retirement years, attracted by Michigan's nature and beauty.

POPULATION DENSITY

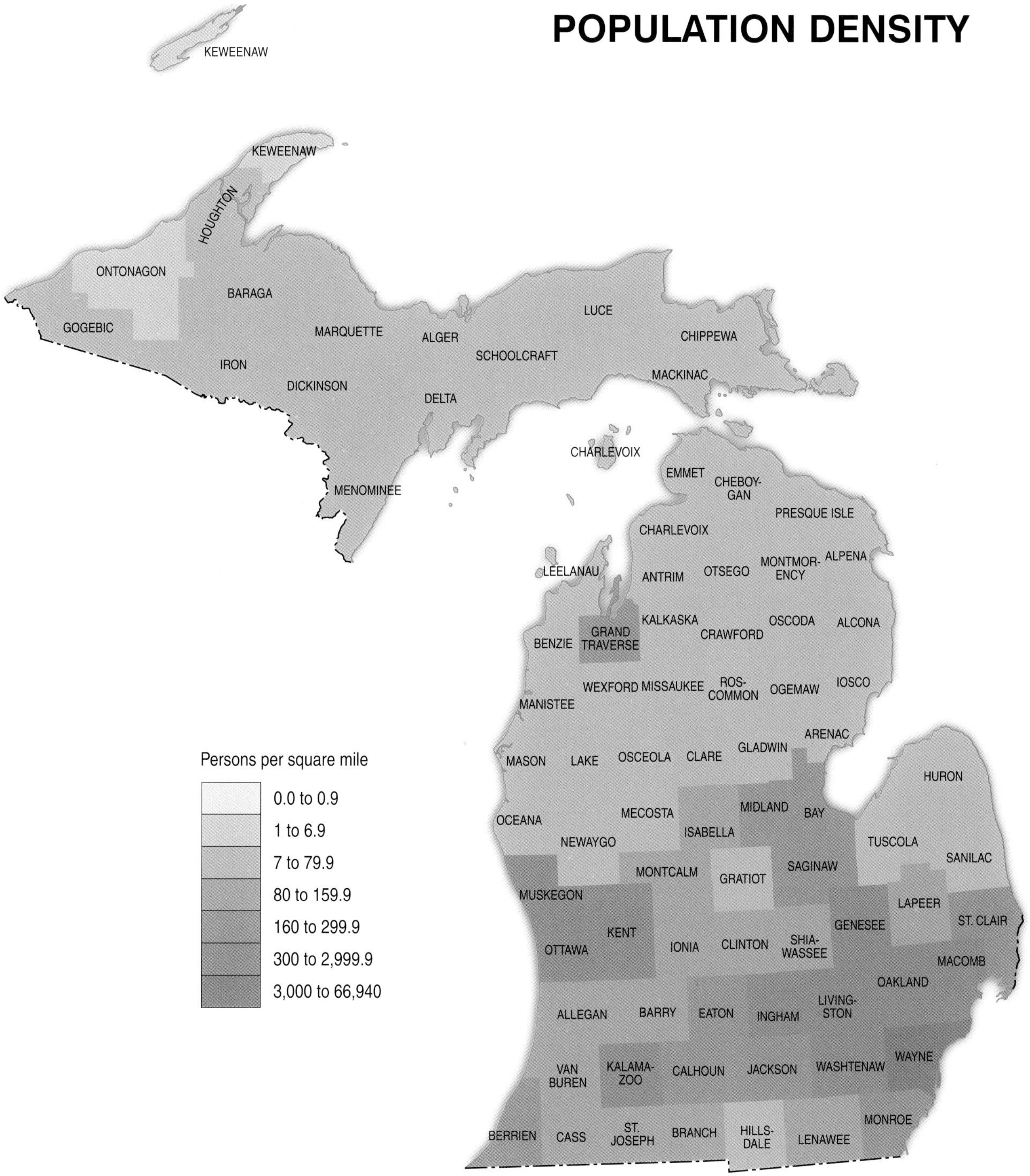
KEWEENAW
KEWEENAW
HOUGHTON
ONTONAGON
BARAGA
GOGEBIC
MARQUETTE
ALGER
LUCE
CHIPPEWA
SCHOOLCRAFT
IRON
DICKINSON
DELTA
MACKINAC
CHARLEVOIX
MENOMINEE
EMMET
CHEBOY-GAN
PRESQUE ISLE
CHARLEVOIX
LEELANAU
ANTRIM
OTSEGO
MONTMOR-ENCY
ALPENA
KALKASKA
GRAND TRAVERSE
BENZIE
CRAWFORD
OSCODA
ALCONA
WEXFORD
MISSAUKEE
ROS-COMMON
OGEMAW
IOSCO
MANISTEE
ARENAC
MASON
LAKE
OSCEOLA
CLARE
GLADWIN
HURON
OCEANA
MECOSTA
MIDLAND
BAY
NEWAYGO
ISABELLA
TUSCOLA
SANILAC
MONTCALM
GRATIOT
SAGINAW
MUSKEGON
LAPEER
ST. CLAIR
GENESEE
KENT
OTTAWA
IONIA
CLINTON
SHIA-WASSEE
MACOMB
OAKLAND
ALLEGAN
BARRY
EATON
INGHAM
LIVING-STON
WAYNE
VAN BUREN
KALAMA-ZOO
CALHOUN
JACKSON
WASHTENAW
MONROE
BERRIEN
CASS
ST. JOSEPH
BRANCH
HILLS-DALE
LENAWEE
Persons per square mile
0.0 to 0.9
1 to 6.9
7 to 79.9
80 to 159.9
160 to 299.9
300 to 2,999.9
3,000 to 66,940

BIG TOWNS, LITTLE TOWNS

Michigan's 2005 population was 10,120,860 people. More than 80 percent of Michiganders still live in urban areas. Most occupy the southern half of the Lower Peninsula. The difference now is that more big-city folk keep moving farther into outlying suburbs.

Detroit remains Michigan's largest city, with a population of 911,402 people. But that figure has dropped by 7.5 percent since 1990. Even so, Detroit ranks as the nation's ninth-largest metropolitan area with 4,452,557 people, including those living in nearby suburbs.

The city is working to attract more people. Riverfront arenas bring sports-lovers downtown regularly. Three downtown casinos offer late-night entertainment. In 1987 the city built the People Mover, an elevated train that links sports, convention, and concert venues with hotels, offices, and shopping areas. The train also goes to the block-long Greektown area near downtown and Bricktown, a neighborhood of historic brick buildings.

Many Michiganders feel that these projects are too few and too scattered to make much of a difference. There are still many boarded grand downtown buildings in the city. One in three people live in poverty in Detroit. Homeless folks sleep under the expressway. But these problems worry the governments of several large cities.

Efforts to bolster Detroit's downtown continue. Scattered housing projects brighten the industrial riverfront. The state government offers grants to groups that want to redevelop city neighborhoods as part of the "Cool Cities" project. The real growth, however, has been in nearby Royal Oak and neighboring Ferndale. These suburbs boast a mix of trendy coffeehouses, restaurants, and dance clubs designed to attract young people with their lively nightlife.

Detroit's downtown attracts diners to an outdoor restaurant.

ETHNIC MICHIGAN

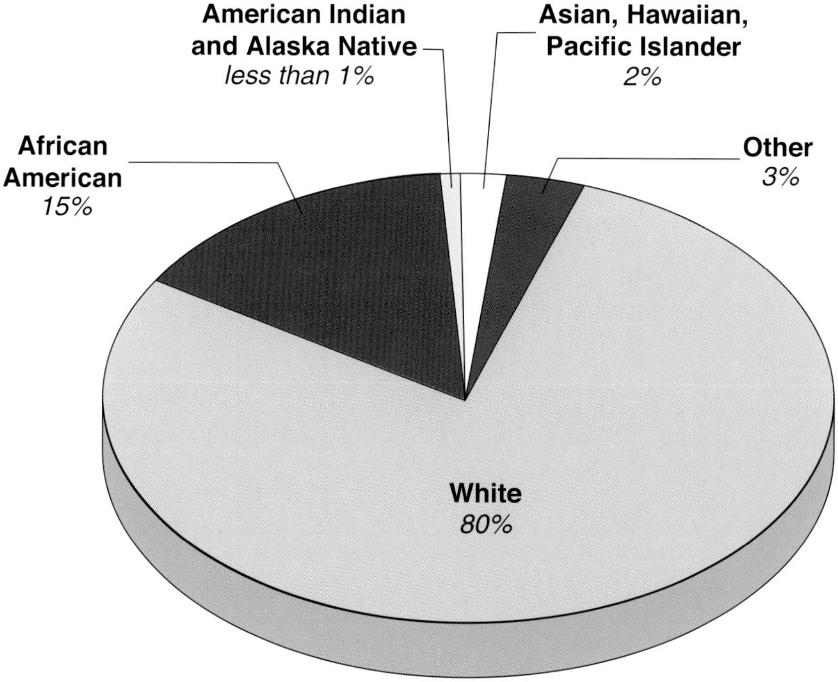
American Indian
and Alaska Native
less than 1%
Asian, Hawaiian,
Pacific Islander
2%
African
American
15%
Other
3%
White
80%

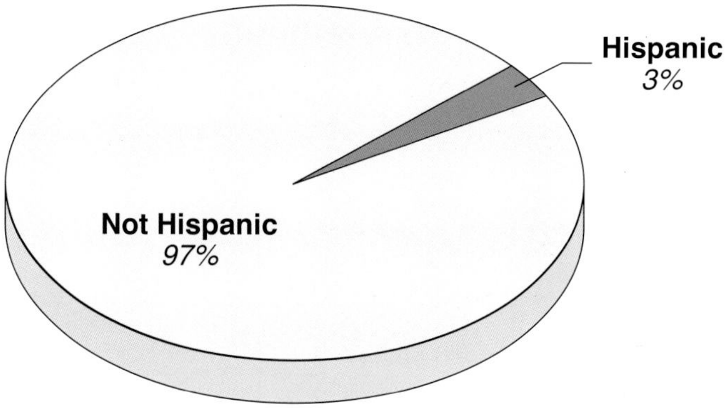
Hispanic
3%
Not Hispanic
97%

Note: A person of Cuban, Mexican, Puerto Rican, South or Central American, or other Spanish culture or origin, regardless of race, is defined as Hispanic.

THE WORLD COMES TO MICHIGAN

Michigan's population includes more than forty nationalities that settled in large numbers during the nineteenth and twentieth centuries. Today, the greatest numbers claim ancestors from Mexico, Poland, Greece, the Middle East, France, Germany, Italy, and Korea. That means visitors can feast on everything from fried goat cheese, called *saganaki*, in Detroit's Greektown to Polish sausage in Hamtramck to Cornish pasties (meat pies) in the Upper Peninsula. So many ethnic groups enrich Michigan that Detroit holds annual riverfront festivals to celebrate different ethnic groups. Festivals highlight foods, music, dances in native costume, and crafts from different cultures.

Michigan's largest group comes from across the border in Canada. Many Canadians cross the border daily for their jobs and then return at night. Another major group includes people whose ancestors came from Finland. Finlandia College in the Upper Peninsula is the largest Finnish college outside of Finland. "We also have one of the largest Finnish populations in the United States outside of Minnesota," the Upper Penninsula's Eric Bourdo boasts.

More recently, immigrants from Latin America, Asia, and the Middle East have built large communities in Michigan. The Hispanic population comprises 3 percent of Michigan's population, a huge increase from a decade ago.

Michigan has one of the fastest-growing Arab communities in the nation. According to the 2000 U.S. census, the number of Arabs jumped from 0.8 percent in 1990 to 1.2 percent of the state's population in 2000. Riverside has a huge mosque, and many Arabs live in Sterling Heights, Warren, and Livonia. Thirty percent of Dearborn's 100,000 residents identify themselves as Arab Americans.

The largest number is Lebanonese. So many residents of Arab descent live in Michigan that their community opened the Arab American National Museum in Dearborn. The 38,500-square-foot museum "honors their past and their identity."

Michigan has a growing Arab community. This student studies at the American Islamic Academy.

CEAD MILLE FAILTE
(ONE HUNDRED THOUSAND WELCOMES IN SCOTTISH)

Where can you find boys in skirts, collie sheepherding, and thirty bagpipe bands? At the Scottish Highland Festival in Alma, of course. Each May the central Lower Peninsula comes alive with music, parades, dancing, and Highland games to honor Alma's Scottish heritage. The festival is one of the nation's major "gathering of clans."

At the festival, dancers compete to Scottish tunes. Some athletes use pitchforks to throw 25-pound bean sacks over a bar. Others toss 20-foot-long logs as thick as telephone poles into the air.

"What's really neat is the 'gathering of the bands' in kilts, horsehair hats, and tartan plaids to represent each clan. Colorful drummers and bagpipers fill an entire football field," visitor Robin Campbell said.

"I even joined the Campbell society," Chesser, her husband, an Illinois Scotsman, added.

The state's largest nonwhite minority is made up of African Americans, who comprise 15 percent of the population. Most live near industrial areas, especially Detroit. Michigan has been home to some of the nation's most outspoken civil rights leaders. One of the boldest black leaders to emerge from Michigan inner cities was Coleman Young, Detroit's first black mayor. The tough-talking mayor saw the city through its stormiest days. He served from 1973 to 1994 and was reelected an amazing five times.

ARTIN LUTHER KING JR.
YOUTH
PEACE MAKERS
"KEEP THE DREAM ALIVE"

Martin Luther King Jr. Youth Peace Makers march during the Martin Luther King Jr. Day parade.

Civil rights leader JoAnn Watson said, "He's the only mayor I've known whom the brothers . . . slap hands and say, 'My man.'"

Malcolm X championed international black rights. As a troubled youth in Lansing, Malcolm Little knew firsthand the hatred of some whites for blacks. His father was killed for urging blacks to end white injustice by returning to Africa. After landing in jail for robbery, Malcolm discovered the Muslim religion and racial pride. Out of jail, Malcolm devoted himself to spreading Islam and preaching violence against whites. He changed his last name to X, explaining that it reflected his lost African family name, rather than the family's slave name. In 1964 Malcolm had a change of heart.

He formed the Organization of Afro-American Unity and called for blacks worldwide to join him in the fight against racism. He had come to believe that prejudice hurt both whites and blacks. On February 21, 1965, Malcolm was shot, like his father, for speaking his mind.

KINGS, QUEENS, AND CHURCHES

Religion in Michigan mirrors the state's ethnic mix. Roman Catholics maintain large congregations, and a considerable number of Michiganders follow Protestant, Muslim, and Jewish faiths. Seventh-day Adventists built a large congregation in Battle Creek, and small groups of Amish, Mennonites, and Mormons live in Kent and Ottawa counties. But large cities, such as Detroit, Grand Rapids, and Bay City, support a range of religions.

Roman Catholic worshippers pray during a prayer vigil for the late pope John Paul II.

Smaller towns, such as Holland, offer fewer religious choices. Many of Holland's residents are of Dutch descent. The town boasts a wooden shoe factory and the only operating Dutch windmill in the United States. The Dutch Reformed Church has dominated Holland since the town was settled in 1847. Holland's Hope College provides education mixed with church teachings. "If you're Catholic like I am, you feel the Dutch Reformed Church everywhere," Steve Eighmey said. "Everyone is open and friendly. But dating can be rough. Parents say 'No way!'"

Michigan has had its share of unusual religions. In 1847 James Strang proclaimed himself "King of Beaver Island," an island northwest of Charlevoix. Strang believed that God had told him to establish a strict Mormon community called Saint James Village and to take several wives. Some of Strang's followers hated his tight control and he was shot in 1856. All that remains of Saint James Village is the Old Mormon Print Shop built by "King Strang."

In 1903 Benjamin Franklin Purnell declared himself king, too. King Ben founded the Israelite House of David in Benton Harbor. Six hundred followers lived and worked together and combined their earnings. They practiced Purnell's strict teachings without smoking, drinking, or eating meat. Purnell's death in 1927 caused the religion to split into two rival sects. His wife, Mary, established the new Israelite City of David and proclaimed herself queen. Judge Harry Dewhirst led the original group. Both branches survive to this day.

SCHOOL CHOICES

The newest password to education for Michiganders is *choice*. From big cities to the rural Upper Peninsula, state lawmakers want schools to be tailored to students and their families.

The idea of choice has created competition between public, religious, and privately run charter schools. In 2004 Michigan enrolled students in 825 public schools, 533 parochial schools, and 989 home schools. Public schools see choice as a challenge, because money earmarked for education follows the student. If too many children leave public schools, these institutions would be unable to exist. So public school administrators across the state devised creative options for students.

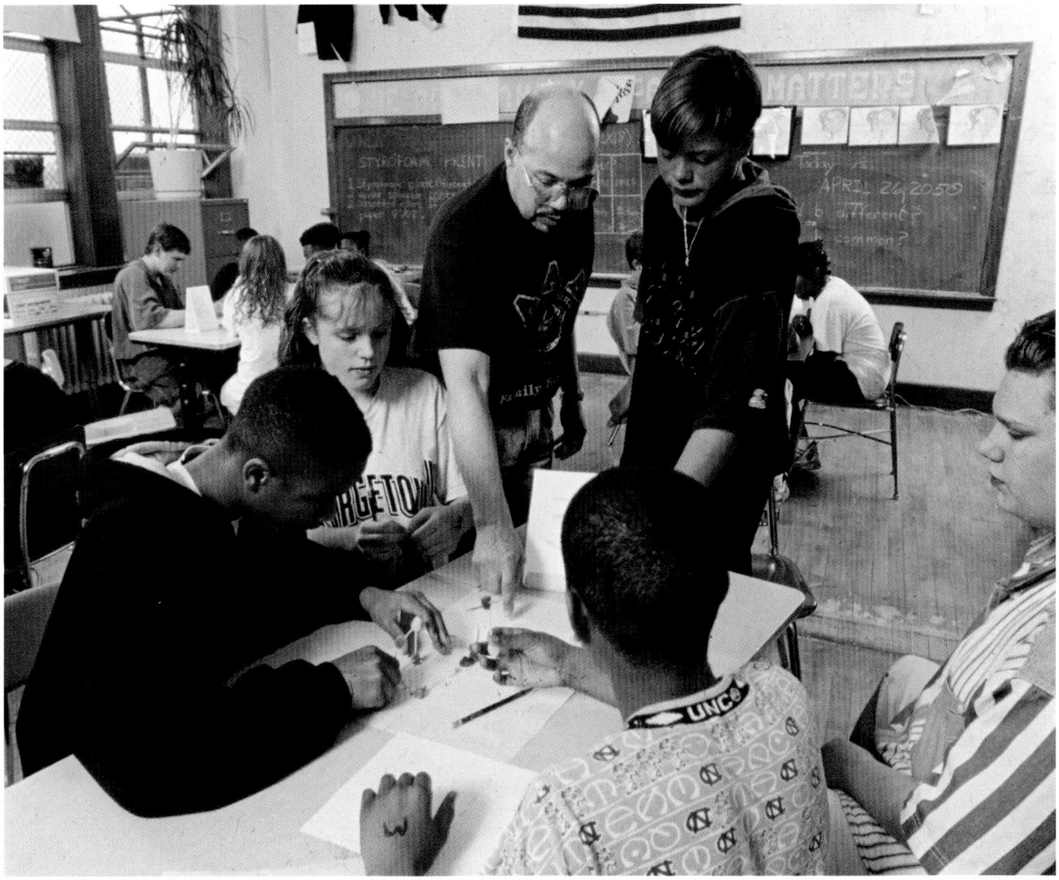
MATTERS
UNC

Michigan's State Board of Education strives "to create learning environments that prepare students to be successful in the twenty-first century."

Dearborn public schools, for example, developed a "Theme Schools and Academies Program." The program gave individual schools the freedom to develop centers that focus on specific offerings, such as creative arts, engineering, or history. The program was a hit. Instead of losing students, Dearborn's enrollment increased.

As happens nationwide, crime, drugs, and uneven teaching affect Michigan schools. Most downtown Detroit schools have police on campus. Even with changes that brought more choice, about one in ten Michigan families sends their children to private schools. Most often, the students go to parochial schools. More than half of religious schools are Roman Catholic.

Two of Michigan's private schools offer some of the most exciting opportunities anywhere in the nation. Cranbrook Educational Community is an art- and science-lover's paradise. Its lovely campus in Bloomfield Hills is home to live-in elementary and high school students and excellent science and art museums that are open to the public. Cranbrook has attracted famous sculptors, architects, and scientists as teachers. Eliel Saarinen, a Finnish architect, designed Cranbrook, as well as countless trendsetting buildings. His renowned son Eero created the Saint Louis arch and many world-class buildings and furniture designs. Eero died in 1961 in Ann Arbor, leaving many creations on Cranbrook's grounds and around Detroit.

Another Michigan treasure is Interlochen Arts Academy. Nestled in the forests of the northwest Lower Peninsula, Interlochen is one of the foremost high schools for performing and visual arts. Each summer, boys and girls of all ages can attend overnight camp. The program blends outdoor fun with music, writing, acting, dancing, conducting, and painting. "For me, Interlochen was the joy of finding a heart . . . in music shared," said singer Peter Yarrow of the folk group Peter, Paul, and Mary.

A student at the Interlochen Arts Academy weaves at her loom.

I.M. Sports Circle
Museum-Union-Library
Hannah Administration
Computer Center
Agriculture Hall
Auditorium - Fairchild
Kresge Art Center
Chapel
Music Building

Michigan State University offers more than two hundred programs of study for the more than 40,000 enrolled students.

HIGHER EDUCATION

Michigan has always had a strong tradition of higher education. The state was first in the nation to establish a college of agriculture at Michigan State in tree-lined East Lansing. It also opened the first college for training teachers west of the Alleghenies, Eastern Michigan University in Ypsilanti. These colleges, plus the highly rated University of Michigan in Ann Arbor, draw tens of thousands of college students from around the world.

Northern Michigan University at Marquette is the only college to boast a United States Olympic Education Center. The center is home to athletes training for biathlon, boxing, cross-country skiing, luge, and short-track speed-skating. Students receive world-class preparation to capture Olympic honors while earning a degree. At the 2006 Winter Olympics in Italy, a women's hockey team from the center won a bronze medal. Cheney Haight captured the gold in wrestling, and Valerie Fleming earned the silver medal for bobsledding. Valerie always said, "I'm going to the Olympics [even] if I have to walk [there]."

A program known as the Kalamazoo Promise makes higher education available to any student in the city's public school system. This unusual program, the only one of its kind in the nation, pays for students to attend any Michigan four-year college after high school. To qualify, students must keep at least a 2.0 grade point average during high school and be enrolled in Kalamazoo schools for at least four years. High school junior Ashley Hill told a local reporter, "We needed this. A lot of us going to college weren't going to because of funds."

Chapter Four

Inside Government

Michigan's government is divided into three branches: executive, legislative, and judicial. Each branch has different jobs. The branches also have powers to check each other, making sure lawmakers provide balanced government.

EXECUTIVE BRANCH

Every four years, Michiganders elect a governor to head the executive branch. Michigan's governor supervises nineteen departments, appoints hundreds of people to boards and committees, vetoes (rejects) or signs bills into law, and plans the state budget.

In 2002 Jennifer Granholm became Michigan's forty-seventh governor. Granholm inherited a state that was deep in debt and losing jobs. She made balancing the budget and growing the state economy her top priorities. But she did not want to balance the budget by cutting programs for children and the poor.

Within two years, Granholm found seven companies to build new headquarters in Michigan and helped thousands of small businesses open by

Michigan's State Capitol has been the seat of the state's government since its completion in 1879.

reducing rules that scared off new owners. Even with these efforts, job loss continued. In 2005 Michigan was the only state, other than hurricane-damaged Mississippi and Louisiana, to list more job losses than jobs created.

Granholm's real successes came in social programs. She restored funding to schools, introduced plans to provide health care to more citizens, and legislated to protect senior citizens in nursing homes. Her plan to cover more children with health insurance added 50,000 people to state health plans. As a result, *Governing Magazine* gave Granholm and Michigan high marks for how they care for people.

Governor Jennifer Granholm's top priorities are "growing Michigan's economy and maintaining the state's high quality of life."

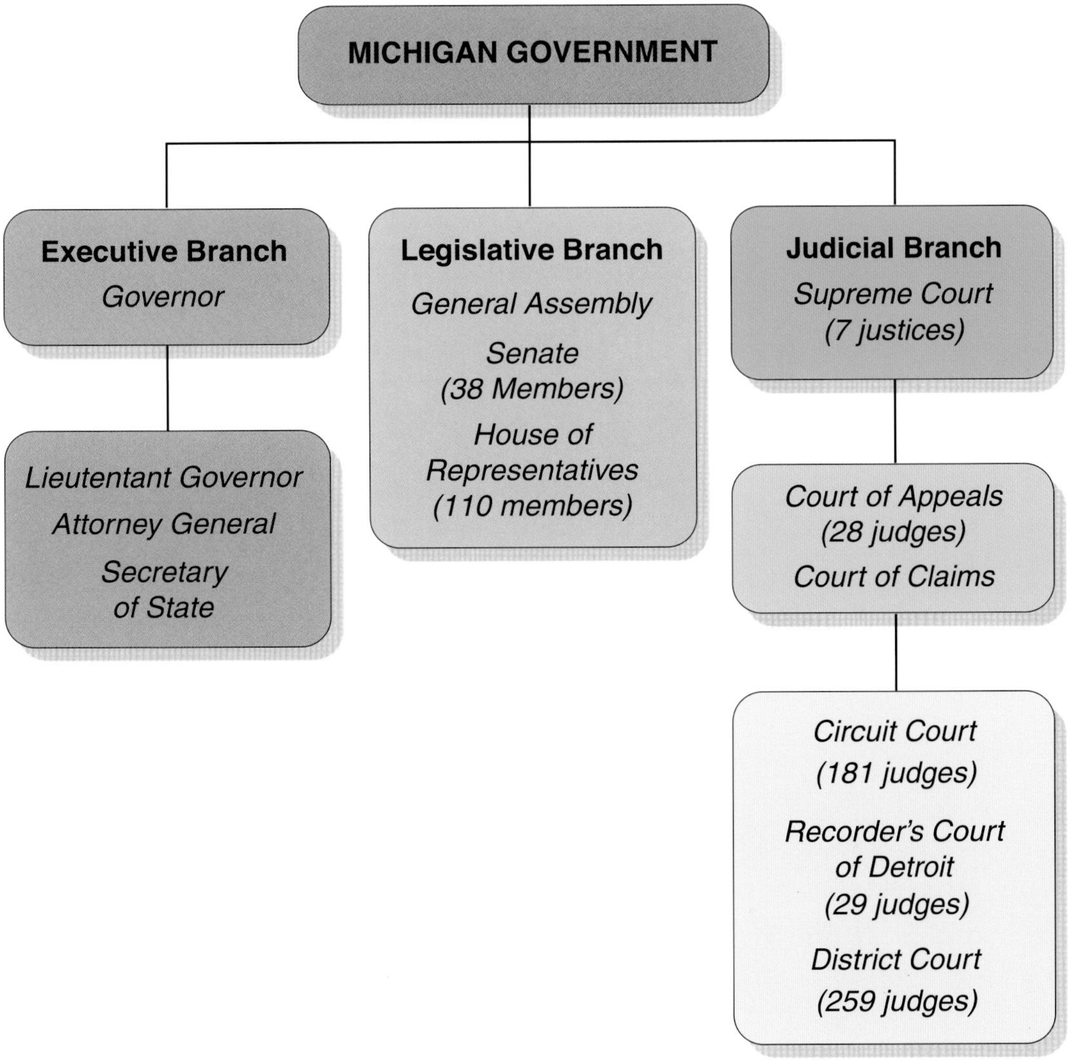
MICHIGAN GOVERNMENT
Executive Branch
Governor
Lieutentant Governor
Attorney General
Secretary of State
Legislative Branch
General Assembly
Senate (38 Members)
House of Representatives (110 members)
Judicial Branch
Supreme Court (7 justices)
Court of Appeals (28 judges)
Court of Claims
Circuit Court (181 judges)
Recorder's Court of Detroit (29 judges)
District Court (259 judges)

LEGISLATIVE BRANCH

Michigan's legislature is divided into two chambers: the Senate and the House of Representatives. Thirty-eight senators are elected to four-year terms. The 110 representatives are elected for two-year terms. Each represents residents of a particular district around the state.

Michigan's legislatures enact laws, propose amendments, as well as oversee the executive branch of the government.

The legislature spends most of its time creating laws. During a two-year term, legislative lawmakers consider between three thousand and four thousand bills that may or may not become law. Bills can originate in either chamber, but they need the approval of both chambers to become law. Once both chambers agree, the bill goes to the governor to sign into law or veto. A vetoed bill can still become law if two-thirds of the legislature vote to overturn the governor's veto.

JUDICIAL BRANCH

Michigan has a many-layered court system. The highest court is the state supreme court. Seven judges rule on cases for eight-year terms.

Hundreds of judges on several levels of lower courts serve specific towns, districts, or types of cases.

Most cases begin in local trial courts, mainly in district court. Michigan has one hundred district courts with judges who are elected for six-year terms. Judges hear criminal cases; civil cases, such as those about money or landlord-tenant arguments; and many traffic violations. Anyone who is seventeen or over can present a case in district court. Children must be represented by an adult in special juvenile courts.

RIGHT TO DIE

Some people in politics view Michigan as a trendsetter. In the state's early days, presidents listened to lumber and auto barons before making decisions. During the late 1990s, the nation watched a retired seventy-nine-year-old Royal Oak doctor named Jack Kevorkian face a different sort of challenge.

Kevorkian fought for the right of very ill patients to choose to die on their own terms and for the right of doctors to help them die painlessly. Between 1990 and 1999, Kevorkian helped more than 130 people die. In response, the state enacted a law against doctor-assisted suicide. Town, state, and national lawyers tried to stop Kevorkian in three costly trials. Each time, juries refused to convict him.

Dr. Jack Kevorkian was charged with murder for overseeing the assisted death of one of his patients.

In 1998 Kevorkian helped a man with a deadly disease die while being filmed for CBS's *60 Minutes.* Michigan courts charged Kevorkian with second-degree murder based on evidence from the television show. A judge sentenced him to ten to twenty-five years in prison without parole until 2007.

Now Kevorkian seems to have been largely forgotten behind bars. But he opened a door that can never be closed. Since he went to jail, the state of Oregon has passed a law that allows individuals the choice to end their lives, and two other states are considering right-to-die laws.

TWO STATES

Most Michiganders feel a strong community bond. Sometimes, local loyalties divide the state. People in the Upper Peninsula feel their interests differ greatly from those in the Lower Peninsula. Every few years Upper Peninsula lawmakers suggest that they should form a separate state. They even thought of a name: Superior.

When efforts to split from Michigan fail, some talk of joining Wisconsin. Many from the Upper Peninsula feel they have more in common with their neighbor than with the rest of Michigan. They claim that residents of Wisconsin and the Upper Peninsula share a quiet, small-town feeling and value their natural surroundings, unlike people in the Lower Peninsula's manufacturing towns. "We have a sportsmen's ethic up here," said Harry Hill, of the Michigan Wildlife Division. "We appreciate nature, being outdoors and sharing and harvesting animals in a fair chase."

The Michigan state government cares about its people. Lawmakers enact some laws to attract business, while passing others to preserve the state's beauty and natural resources. At the same time, judges work to keep Michiganders in the Lower and Upper peninsulas safe and living in harmony.

MICHIGAN BY COUNTY

KEWEENAW
KEWEENAW
HOUGHTON
ONTONAGON
BARAGA
GOGEBIC
MARQUETTE
ALGER
LUCE
CHIPPEWA
SCHOOLCRAFT
IRON
MACKINAC
DICKINSON
DELTA
CHARLEVOIX
MENOMINEE
EMMET
CHEBOY-
GAN
PRESQUE ISLE
CHARLEVOIX
LEELANAU
ANTRIM
OTSEGO
MONTMOR-
ENCY
ALPENA
KALKASKA
GRAND
TRAVERSE
BENZIE
CRAWFORD
OSCODA
ALCONA
WEXFORD
MISSAUKEE
ROS-
COMMON
OGEMAW
IOSCO
MANISTEE
ARENAC
MASON
LAKE
OSCEOLA
CLARE
GLADWIN
HURON
OCEANA
MECOSTA
MIDLAND
BAY
NEWAYGO
ISABELLA
TUSCOLA
SANILAC
MONTCALM
GRATIOT
SAGINAW
MUSKEGON
LAPEER
ST. CLAIR
GENESEE
KENT
OTTAWA
IONIA
CLINTON
SHIA-
WASSEE
MACOMB
OAKLAND
ALLEGAN
BARRY
EATON
INGHAM
LIVING-
STON
WAYNE
VAN
BUREN
KALAMA-
ZOO
CALHOUN
JACKSON
WASHTENAW
MONROE
BERRIEN
CASS
ST.
JOSEPH
BRANCH
HILLS-
DALE
LENAWEE

KELLEY

Chapter Five

Automobiles and Beyond

Michigan's economy has been up and down. During the 1980s, the state's economy went into a tailspin. As the auto industry declined, so did industries that supplied its raw materials. Jobs were lost, and with them the salaries needed to buy food and goods and keep the economy moving.

Over the next decade, Michiganders fought to climb out of the slump. Many towns found the struggle to revive factory, farm, and service jobs worth the effort. Between 1994 and 1999, Michigan's jobless rate fell below the national average for the first time in thirty years, and Michigan ended the 1990s with a more diverse economy. According to *The Almanac of American Politics*, Michigan is "a laboratory of economic transformation, helping show America how to move from an industrial to postindustrial economy."

By 2000 the economy showed signs of reversing. Unemployment rates crept upward again. The numbers showed that Michigan had higher unemployment rates than the rest of the nation. That gap has held steady for several years.

More than 40 percent of Michigan's workforce is in the service sector. This worker prepares fruit trays for a gourmet food retailer in Detroit.

CHALLENGES FOR THE NEW CENTURY

Today the largest share of Michigan's labor force, 42 percent, is in the service sector. Jobs in education, health, and social services account for 21 percent of service workers. Manufacturing employs 20 percent of the workforce. Although sales positions offer the greatest share of jobs, manufacturing brings in the largest amount of state income.

In 2006 General Motors and Ford announced cuts in Michigan factories and jobs, threatening state and workers incomes once again. Shoppers wanted smaller foreign cars that ran on less fuel. American carmakers had thought the public wanted larger, gas-guzzling sport utility vehicles. They were caught unprepared for the buyer's change of heart. To survive, companies cut costs. With the production of fewer automobiles, companies that supplied car parts suffered as well. Hardest hit were Detroit and Flint. Detroit's unemployment rate stood at 7 percent, compared with the nation's 5 percent.

Michigan's automakers produced many truck and sport utility vehicles in an attempt to supply buyer's needs. However, smaller vehicles are now in demand due to the high cost of gasoline.

Governor Granholm made replacing lost jobs her top priority. Once unheard of for Michigan, she courted Toyota, the Japanese company that was set to overtake Michigan's General Motors as the world's biggest carmaker. Granholm brought one Toyota plant to Michigan and wants more.

She also set out to improve education. Less than 25 percent of Michigan residents earn a college degree, and many lack high school degrees. One reason for the lack of diplomas is that workers have traditionally relied on good-paying jobs in auto plants. But that is changing. According to a recent Millennium Project report, "Michigan's old manufacturing economy is dying. . . . Economic shifts are putting at risk the welfare of millions of citizens of our state in the face of withering competition from an emerging global knowledge economy."

MICHIGAN WORKFORCE

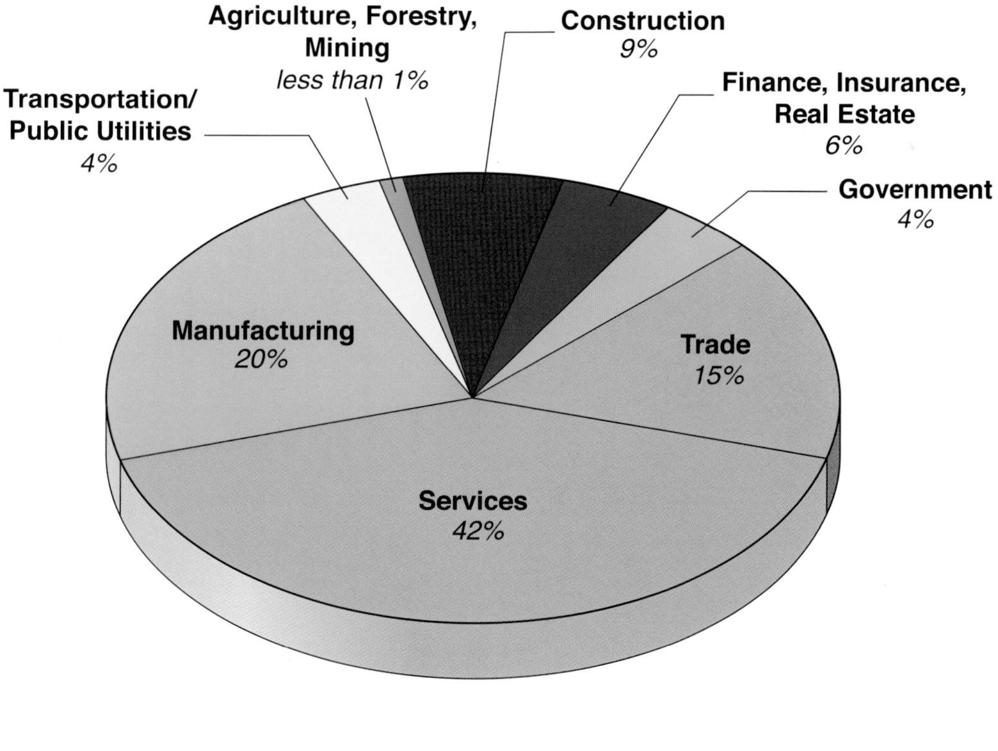
Agriculture, Forestry, Mining
less than 1%
Construction
9%
Finance, Insurance, Real Estate
6%
Government
4%
Trade
15%
Services
42%
Manufacturing
20%
Transportation/ Public Utilities
4%

MORE THAN CARS

Now, in the twenty-first century, only one-fifth of the state's manufacturing involves motor vehicles. Michigan has the nation's largest office furniture industry and also has strong medicine and medical supply, chemical, food processing, and machinery-building businesses.

Michigan also discovered another natural growth area in recycling. Several paper mills and printers using Michigan lumber are operated in the Upper Peninsula. Once the lumber was gone, printers looked for cheaper and more plentiful fiber. As far back as the 1950s, companies began converting used newsprint into usable paper.

9200B
POT
Located in Midland, the Dow Chemical Company is the largest chemical company in the world.

Today, almost any paper product can be recycled in the Upper Peninsula. "In 1990, we overcame the myth that magazines and catalogs don't recycle well," said Eric Bourdo of Manistique Papers. "We are the nation's largest recycler of catalogs and magazines recovered from offices and homes. The best thing is we sit in one of the most heavily forested places in the United States, and we don't use any woods for any of our envelopes, bags, or fast-food tray liners."

Some of Michigan's oldest companies have modernized and

developed new products. Gerber Baby Foods and Kellogg and Post cereals tempt customers with new taste treats regularly. Dr. John Kellogg and his brother, Will, first invented flaked corn cereal for their Battle Creek health spa in 1898. Recently, Kellogg opened a new research center to study food and health. To honor its cereal tradition, in 1956, Battle Creek began hosting the World's Longest Breakfast Table every second Saturday in June. Today, more than 60,000 guests down about 4,500 pounds of cereal and 40,000 pounds of bananas during each festival.

Kellogg's CORN FLAKES
Kellogg's
CORN
FLAKES
The Original and Best

Battle Creek is the home to Kellogg's, the world leader in cereal production. The company's established sales are more than nine billion dollars.

FUN FAIR DAYS

Michigan has the nation's oldest state fair. But that doesn't mean it's the tamest. Imagine being shot 70 feet into the air in a giant rubber band called the Ejection Seat, or winning blue ribbons for the craziest parent call. Each year, two weeks before Labor Day, half a million visitors thrill to these and other exciting events at the Michigan State Fair in Detroit.

The first state fair opened in 1849 to help farmers and industrial workers learn more about each other's products. Modern fairs added entertainment, children's events, and livelier displays to the program. Today, children raise show animals and enter contests to see who has the biggest gum bubble or the longest ponytail. Major automakers exhibit the latest car models in addition to farm equipment. In 2005 they added a Car and Truck Swap Meet to display cars from the 1950s and 1960s.

"A favorite is the 'Miracle of Life' birthing exhibit," says Laurie Marrocco, the fair's assistant manager. "Visitors see live chicks, lambs, pigs, and cows being born almost every day at the fair."

2004 GROSS STATE PRODUCT: $327 Million

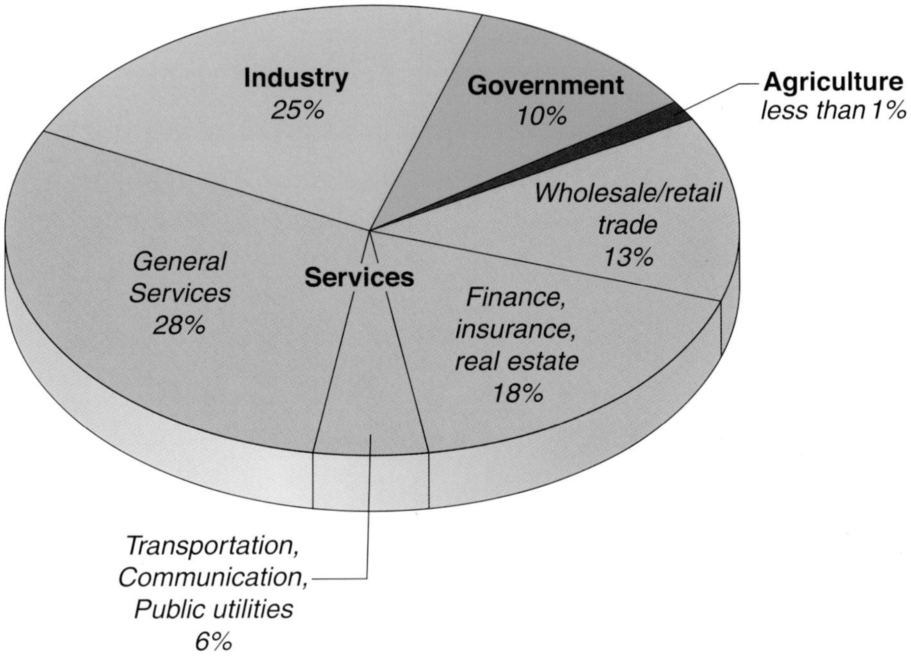
Industry
25%
Government
10%
Agriculture
less than 1%
Wholesale/retail
trade
13%
General
Services
28%
Services
Finance,
insurance,
real estate
18%
Transportation,
Communication,
Public utilities
6%

FROM PLANTS TO FOOD

Michigan is second in the nation for the variety of products it grows. One-third of these products leave the state as exports. The middle Lower Peninsula and thumb regions produce the nation's largest supply of black and navy beans and cranberries. Kalamazoo, once known as Celery Flats, now grows potted plants, since the soil has lost some nutrients. Thousands of geraniums and Easter lilies travel cross-country to celebrations each year.

Fruits and vegetables remain Michigan's agricultural lifeblood. Michigan's fruit belt produces the most apples and pears in the country. Farmers grow more blueberries, cherries, and cucumbers in Michigan than anywhere in the world. During the summer, carloads of fruit lovers from Illinois and Indiana cross state borders to "pick their own."

Michigan harvests 75 percent of the nation's tart cherries. Most come from the northwest Lower Peninsula, making Traverse City the nation's cherry capital. Each July, the National Cherry Festival honors the juicy fruit.

Like the rest of the nation, Michigan has experienced a decrease in its number of farms. Unlike in other states, however, Michigan farmers tend to hand down farms from one generation to the next. "Uncle John's apple farm and cider mill is a hundred-year-old family business. Family farms are the norm for nearby mint, bean, and corn fields," said a woman selling cinnamon-laced apple fritters in central Michigan.

Michigan is the top producer of cherries in the United States.

BLUEBERRY JAM

Native Americans collected wild blueberries along Michigan shores long before Europeans even knew the Great Lakes existed. Today, Michigan leads the country in harvesting these juicy fruits. An entire industry developed around manufacturing equipment to harvest and clean blueberries, and it's all found near South Haven.

To celebrate the tasty treat, South Haven holds the National Blueberry Festival. Each August, more than ten thousand visitors watch the Blueberry Parade, complete with Dutch Klompen Dancers from nearby Holland, Michigan, and line dancers doing the Blueberry Shuffle. Kids compete in blueberry pie eating and blueberry bubble gum blowing contests and munch blueberry popcorn. Many take home blueberry plants to grow their own for pancakes, scones, and cereal.

Ask an adult to help you make this recipe for Michigan blueberry jam:

2 1/2 cups blueberries
2 1/4 cups sugar
1/2 cup orange juice
1 tablespoon lemon juice
3 ounces fruit pectin

Wash the blueberries and remove any stems. Place the blueberries in an enamel or stainless steel pan that won't stain and crush the fruit. Add the sugar and fruit juices. Mix well. Boil the mixture for one minute before removing from the heat. Stir in pectin. Pour into sterilized jars. If you can keep from gobbling up the jam, seal the jars for use weeks or months later.

EARNING A LIVING

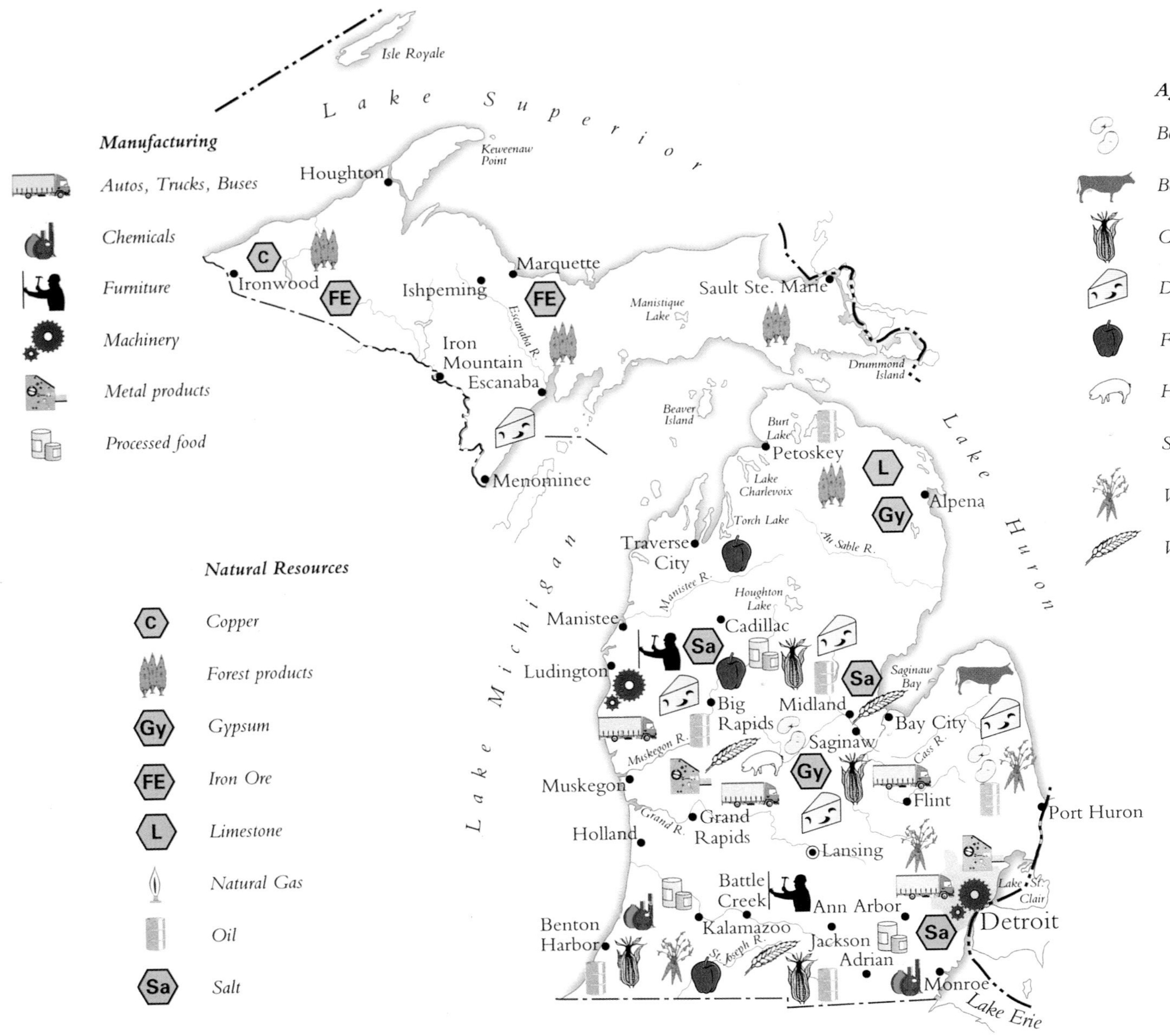
Manufacturing
Autos, Trucks, Buses
Chemicals
Furniture
Machinery
Metal products
Processed food
Natural Resources
Copper
Forest products
Gypsum
Iron Ore
Limestone
Natural Gas
Oil
Salt
Agriculture
Beans
Beef cattle
Corn
Dairy products
Fruit
Hogs
Sugar beets
Vegetables
Wheat
Isle Royale
Lake Superior
Keweenaw Point
Houghton
Ironwood
Ishpeming
Marquette
Escanaba R.
Iron Mountain
Escanaba
Menominee
Manistique Lake
Sault Ste. Marie
Drummond Island
Beaver Island
Burt Lake
Petoskey
Lake Charlevoix
Torch Lake
Alpena
Au Sable R.
Lake Huron
Lake Michigan
Traverse City
Manistee R.
Houghton Lake
Manistee
Cadillac
Ludington
Big Rapids
Midland
Saginaw Bay
Bay City
Saginaw
Cass R.
Muskegon R.
Muskegon
Flint
Port Huron
Grand R.
Grand Rapids
Holland
Lansing
Battle Creek
Ann Arbor
Lake St. Clair
Detroit
Benton Harbor
Kalamazoo
St. Joseph R.
Jackson
Adrian
Monroe
Lake Erie
C
FE
Gy
L
Sa

To keep their farms, many Michigan farmers have to work second jobs. Cindy Dutcher raises chickens and organic vegetables. Besides farming, her husband, John, delivers packages. After farming for ten years, they are beginning to make ends meet. "Lots of times I worked all day in the field and then waited tables in a restaurant. You have to love what you're doing to be a farmer," Dutcher says.

NATURAL RICHES

Much of Michigan's mineral wealth comes from the Upper Peninsula. Once, copper was king. Today, copper ore is too expensive to mine. Instead, iron provides Michigan's chief mineral wealth. The two iron mines in Marquette County alone employ about 1,800 people. Only Minnesota mines more iron in the United States.

The Cleveland Cliffs Iron Ore Mine and Mill employs four thousand people and is the industry leader of iron ore pellets.

Tourism contributes more than $17 million to Michigan's economy .

Construction products add to the state's natural wealth. Michigan supplies much of the country's Portland cement, sand, and gravel. Key cement centers are in Alpena, Charlevoix, Monroe, and Bay counties. Limestone, an ingredient in cement, provides the largest quantities and income of any stones mined in Michigan. Other resources, such as oil, gypsum, and natural gas, add to the state budget.

Tourism holds the greatest promise as a growth industry. Money generated from travelers going to beaches, forests, and parks earned the state more than $17.5 billion in 2004. Once, tourism was limited to summer fun—biking, fishing, and water sports. Then the state developed year-round activities: trout-filled streams, seven million acres for public hunting, winter sports, and city cultural sites. Michigan Tourism created several slogans, including "Great Lakes, Great Times," to promote tourism. Enough money comes from hunting and fishing licenses to fund most state wildlife programs. All Michiganders hope more travelers from other states will visit to learn about the delights of vacationing in Michigan.

Chapter Six

Discovering Michigan

Michigan has a variety of places to visit—children's museums, space museums, parks, factories, lighthouses, and historic homes. Throughout the state, there are pretty hideaway towns and nature areas as well. Exciting places are everywhere in Michigan.

EXPLORING DETROIT

Detroit sits along a river by the same name that connects the United States and Canada. Detroit's founder, Antoine de la Mothe Cadillac, called the region "the earthly paradise of North America." In 1806, Michigan's first judge, Augustus Woodward, honored the beautiful city with the same layout as Washington, D.C. He built major streets extending from the river through a series of plazas, like spokes on a wheel. Today, expressways cut through the grid, leaving a maze of one-way streets.

One of Detroit's liveliest areas is Greektown, especially since a neighborhood casino opened there. Although it is only one block long, its bakeries and restaurants spill around corners. A highlight of Greektown is Trappers Alley. Five buildings that line the alley once housed a fur trading

More than two million people visit Holland, Michigan each year. They are drawn to the town's festivals, beaches, parks, and De Zwaan windmill (left).

GREEKTOWN
CASINO

The 100-year-old neighborhood of Greektown offers visitors many restaurants to experience Greek foods and culture.

company. Now the century-old brick structures contain shops and restaurants around a courtyard.

Belle Isle offers a special view of Detroit and Windsor, Canada, from across the Detroit River. Governor Lewis Cass named the island after his daughter, Isabella, in 1845. During the 1880s, Frederick Olmsted, who designed New York's Central Park, developed the island as a public park. Today, Sunset Drive winds through the thousand-acre park to an aquarium, a conservatory, a zoo, and the Dossin Great Lakes Museum. People fish, jog, and bicycle year-round. In the summer, cars pack the drive, bringing families to swim, golf, and picnic.

A view of Detroit from Belle Isle Park

Many Michigan cities celebrate their farming past with weekly open markets. Detroiters claim that their Eastern Market is the largest farm stand in the nation. Open stalls are surrounded by a couple of square blocks of food warehouses and stores with colorful murals. Every few feet there is a different smell—cinnamon, fish, or onions. Visitors can also grab a favorite Detroit snack—hot dogs and Vernor's ginger ale.

Downtown Detroit honors one of the greatest boxers in history with the Joe Louis Arena. Joe Louis Barrow began boxing in the 1930s under the name Joe Louis. The "Brown Bomber from Detroit" held the heavyweight title from 1937 until 1949. African Americans saw Louis as a symbol of hope during a troubled time in their history. Today, a sculpture representing the boxer's arm and the arena recall his talent.

Just off North Woodward Avenue is the historic home where Berry Gordy Jr. invented the Motown sound. In the 1950s, blacks sang a mix of gospel, rhythm and blues, and popular music in churches and on street corners. Some were lucky enough to cut records. But the companies were owned by whites who made money off their black artists without sharing the profits. Gordy challenged the system with his budding record company, which he named after Detroit's nickname, "Motor City." Within a year, the Miracles' song "Shop Around" earned Gordy his first gold record. Gordy molded other inner-city talent into stars. Stevie Wonder, Smokey Robinson, and Indiana's Michael Jackson and the Jackson Five all received their start in Gordy's Detroit studio, which is open to the public.

The sights and sounds of Detroit's car industry are everywhere. Michigan license plates read "World's Motor Capital." The Cobo Hall conference center holds the annual North American International Auto Show, the nation's largest display of cars.

A gift to the city of Detroit, the Joe Lewis Monument is a 24-foot bronze arm and fist sculpture created by artist Robert Graham.

West on I-94 towers a giant Uniroyal tire. The tire began as a Ferris wheel at the 1964 World's Fair in New York, carrying passengers in its center. Uniroyal moved it in 1966. Now drivers speed by a remodeled tire with fiberglass sidewalls.

UNIROYAL TIRES
ROYAL SEAL
UNIROYAL GOODRICH

The giant Uniroyal tire has become one of the most well known roadside attractions in Michigan.

Invention has always been the hallmark of Michigan's automobile industry. The Henry Ford Museum and Greenfield Village celebrate both. Henry Ford moved about a hundred famous people's homes and workplaces to a 260-acre lot in the suburb of Dearborn, his hometown. He transported the entire New Jersey laboratory where Thomas Edison produced the lightbulb. Ford added a village of craftspeople, a working carousel, and a train. Indoors at the museum, he displayed the first motor wagons, steam engines, and farm equipment. Today, the museum also features a Rouge Factory Tour, an IMAX theater, and the Benson Ford Archives. All celebrate Michigan's inventive spirit.

ART FOR THE PEOPLE

As Michigan's largest city, Detroit is the state's art hub. The Detroit Institute of Art is the heart of the arts community. The museum has wonderful collections of early American painters and African-American paintings, pottery, and weavings. But the artwork that really sets this museum apart is *Detroit Industry*, four murals by Mexican painter Diego Rivera.

Rivera completed the industrial scenes in 1933 with the help of Flint's Stephen Dimitroff. The brightly colored inner-court walls present life in early auto factories. The bold figures and machines are said to be Rivera's finest American work.

When the murals were unveiled, however, they caused an uproar. Newspapers called the murals "un-American," and said they belittled factory work. Clergy disliked a section that showed a child getting a vaccination. They thought the family in the scene looked too much like the Holy Family, and that the scene implied that science would triumph over religion. Art critics, however, praised the paintings, and factory workers loved them. Workers streamed into the museum to admire Rivera's depiction of industrial life. Finally, art was presenting subjects that meant something to everyday laborers.

PLACES TO SEE

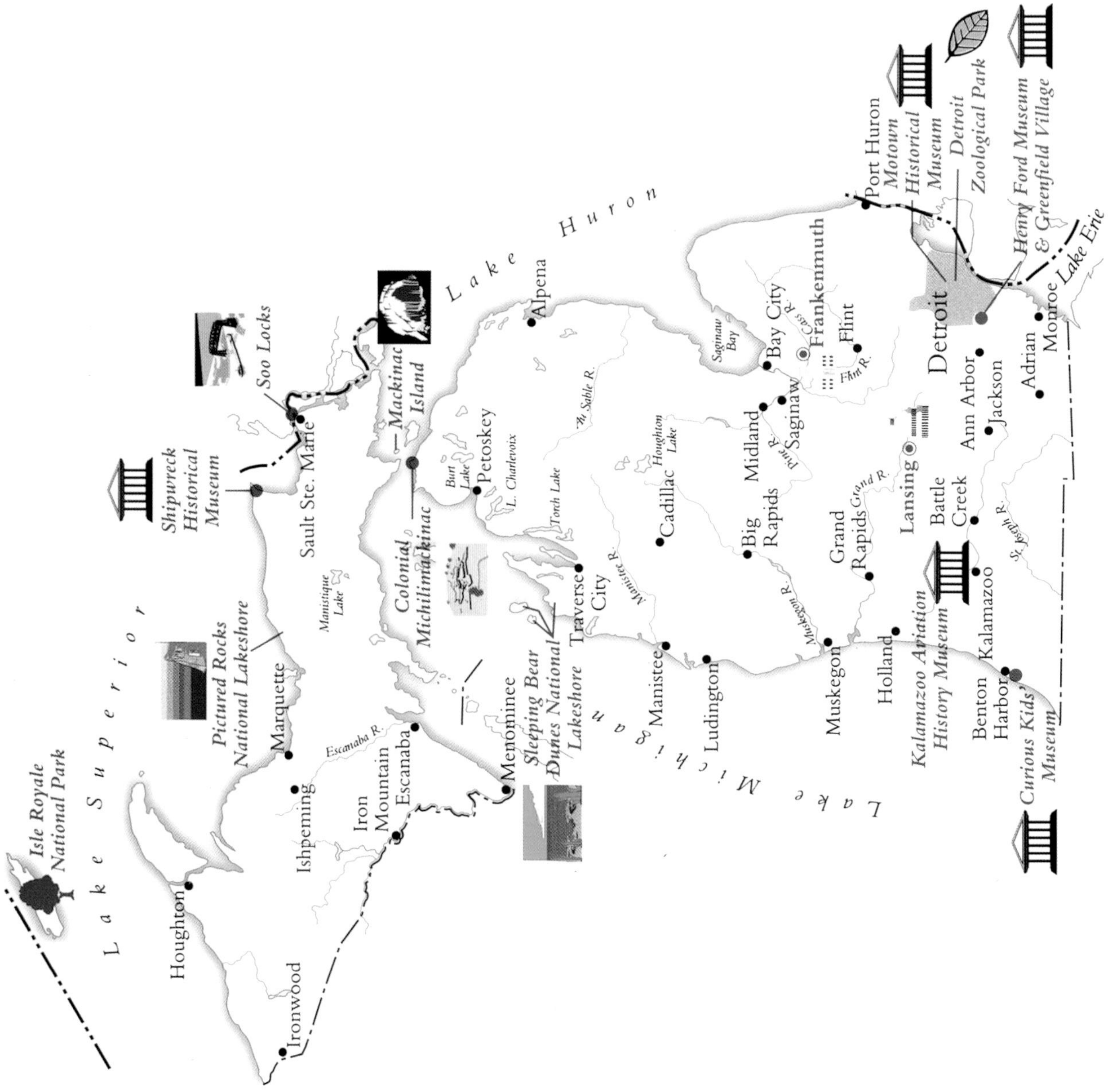
Isle Royale National Park
Lake Superior
Houghton
Ironwood
Ishpeming
Marquette
Pictured Rocks National Lakeshore
Escanaba R.
Iron Mountain
Escanaba
Manistique Lake
Shipwreck Historical Museum
Sault Ste. Marie
Soo Locks
Mackinac Island
Colonial Michilimackinac
Menominee
Sleeping Bear Dunes National Lakeshore
Traverse City
Burt Lake
Petoskey
L. Charlevoix
Torch Lake
Lake Huron
Alpena
Au Sable R.
Houghton Lake
Cadillac
Manistee R.
Manistee
Ludington
Lake Michigan
Big Rapids
Midland
Pine R.
Saginaw
Saginaw Bay
Bay City
Cass R.
Frankenmuth
Flint
Flint R.
Muskegon R.
Muskegon
Grand Rapids
Grand R.
Lansing
Holland
Kalamazoo Aviation History Museum
Battle Creek
Kalamazoo
St. Joseph R.
Benton Harbor
Curious Kids' Museum
Ann Arbor
Jackson
Adrian
Detroit
Monroe
Lake Erie
Port Huron
Motown Historical Museum
Detroit Zoological Park
Henry Ford Museum & Greenfield Village

LOWER PENINSULA CITIES

Many cities throughout Michigan are thriving. With almost 200,000 people, Grand Rapids is Michigan's second-largest city. It was named for the rapids that once bubbled through town in the Grand River. Nearby logging made the forested town famous for producing quality furniture.

Today, a series of dams has replaced the rapids. Between September and October, the five-step Fish Ladder Sculpture helps salmon leap over a six-foot dam on their way to spawn. The sparkly riverfront draws crowds for festivals, and the Gerald Ford Museum highlights its namesake's presidency. A bright red outdoor metal sculpture, *La Grande Vitesse* (The Grand Rapids) by Alexander Calder, pays tribute to the river. The sculpture adds to the downtown's lively mix of old and new buildings and industries.

festival
LA GRANDE VITESSE

On June 14, 1969 La Grande Vittesse *was dedicated to the city of Grand Rapids.*

Midland is the high spot of central Michigan. Midland grew up with Dow Chemical Company in Michigan's heartland. Herbert Dow founded the chemical company in 1897. His experiments led to a variety of everyday products, such as plastic wrap, and pesticides. Today Dow employs 11,000 people locally, with more plants in Japan. The factory is a town in itself, going on for acres and dwarfing Midland's two-block-long downtown.

Herbert Dow has influenced every aspect of the community, bringing theater, music, and the arts to Midland. His son, Alden, made Midland an "architectural island" with the world-class buildings he designed. During his fifty-year career, Alden gave his hometown churches, houses, and a beautiful arts center. Alden's home has been called one of the most beautiful in the United States.

"Midland is the Lower Peninsula's cultural mecca outside Detroit," claimed Detroit's Jackie Pfalzer. "It's a short drive to the wonderful Thumb, where really beautiful lakes and tiny towns haven't lost their old-fashioned charm."

Near Midland, at the mouth of the Saginaw River, is Bay City. During the 1800s, Bay City was the "Lumber Capital of the World." Today, Bay City ranks among the top ports on the Great Lakes. Its harbors handle more tonnage than any port in Michigan besides Detroit. Beyond the sparkling harbor lie a charming downtown and tree-lined neighborhoods with Victorian mansions built by lumber barons. Great fun awaits visitors 5 miles north at the Jennison Nature Center. Here, nature trails and marshland provide homes to a hundred kinds of birds.

Lansing is Michigan's capital and sixth-largest city. State government takes place here in huge marble buildings. The state library and historical museum share wings of one grand building, providing all the information Michiganders might need in one place. The museum houses items such as

AUSTIN BLAIR
WAR GOVERNOR OF MICHIGAN
OF HER CITIZEN SOLDIERS

The State Capitol in Lansing was listed as a National Historic Landmark in 1992.

the state's first cars and a one-room schoolhouse, complete with copies of old student diaries. The capitol is Lansing's most striking building with its tall dome. Michigan was the first state to design a capitol similar to the U.S. Capitol.

Former factories along the Grand River are now museums teeming with happy visitors. The Impression 5 Science Center is the largest of Michigan's many exciting hands-on children's museums. Kids can walk through a giant heart or create magical computer art. Aross the river near a car factory is the Michigan Women's Historical Center & Hall of Fame. This museum celebrates Michigan women from long ago to the present.

Just south of Lansing is the Michigan Space and Science Center in Jackson. The center highlights Michigan's important role in the history of flight. Detroit-born Charles Lindbergh made the first nonstop solo flight across the Atlantic Ocean. His airplane, *Spirit of St. Louis*, soared from New York City to Paris, earning him fans worldwide. Seven Michigan astronauts appear among the exhibits, all graduates of the University of Michigan. Jackson's James McDivitt piloted the spacecraft that carried the first American to walk in outer space. Another Jackson pilot, Alfred Worden, was the command module pilot for Apollo 15. This was the fourth moon landing and the first time astronauts explored mountain ranges on the moon. The center displays a piece of moon rock from that trip.

LAKE MICHIGAN PLAYLAND

For decades, Chicagoans have escaped to western Michigan's resort communities. Artists from every state came to paint the lovely settings at Ox-Bow Lagoon in Saugatuck. Tiny South Haven once claimed more than a hundred resorts. Famous visitors, such as Chicago's mayor Richard Daley and Oprah Winfrey, owned summer homes along the coast. Sand, surf, and shoreline sunrises lured vacationers. Quaint shops and beautiful surroundings kept them coming back.

After a long break, the tourist boom is on again. Homey bed-and-breakfasts have replaced older resorts and cottages. The School of the Art Institute of Chicago operates Ox-Bow, a program where artists go to the lagoon area to paint. Artist colonies dot the coast from South Haven to Saugatuck. Farther north they reappear near the charming resort towns of Charlevoix and Traverse City.

Ed Gray founded an artist's community in Fennville. Gray, an Ojibwe artist, shapes jewelry, fountains, sculptures, and spirit houses from clay and metal. Much of his art is in copper. Gray believes copper is a "healing metal given to native people by the creator." One of Gray's best-known copper designs is for Red Ribbon of Hope. Gray twists the metal into a ribbon-shaped pin that AIDS awareness groups sell to raise money to help care for patients with this deadly disease. Since he began the project in 1992, Gray has produced more than 750,000 pins and raised hundreds of thousands of dollars for AIDS groups nationwide. "People pay what they can for the pin," Gray said. "Sometimes, kids give fifty cents or a dollar. That's exciting when young kids want the ribbon to help fight AIDS."

Besides art, each town along Lake Michigan is proud of its rustic feel and festivals. "You get three people together in Saugatuck, and you can have two parades," a Saugatuck saleswoman joked. "Fennville has a Goose Festival to celebrate the return of 300,000 Canada geese. So we decided to hold a Duck Festival. We have a parade with floats and kids riding bicycles wearing duck bills. It's fun."

TEN LARGEST CITIES

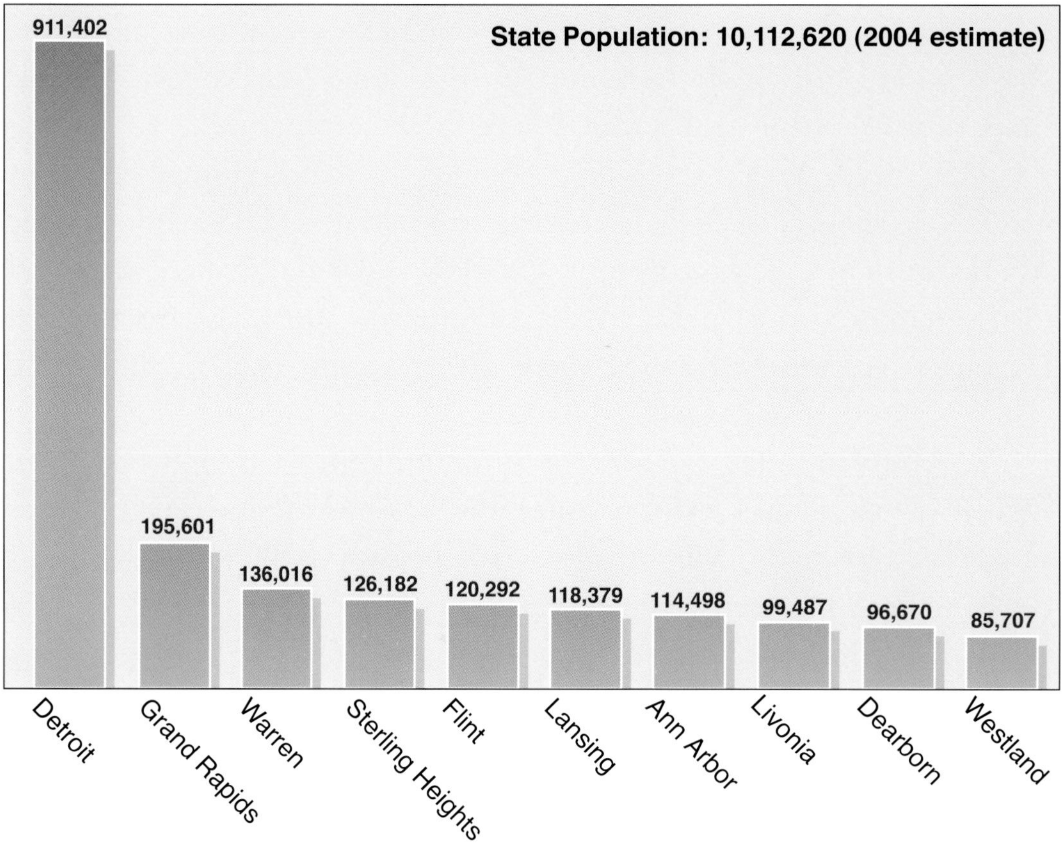

State Population: 10,112,620 (2004 estimate)
911,402
195,601
136,016
126,182
120,292
118,379
114,498
99,487
96,670
85,707
Detroit
Grand Rapids
Warren
Sterling Heights
Flint
Lansing
Ann Arbor
Livonia
Dearborn
Westland

UPPER PENINSULA

"We have everything up here," Jim Swede of Copper Harbor said. "We have natural settings and lots of history. There are beautiful trees and rock formations and water."

Between the Upper and Lower peninsulas is Mackinac Island, "Land of the Great Turtle." The island is Michigan's most popular natural park. Cars are banned, and the only way to reach the island is by ferry. Visitors troop in and out of antique and fudge shops on foot. Residents call tourists "fudgies" because so many stroll along munching fudge.

Mackinac Island Harbor can be viewed best by horse-drawn carriage.

Many people bicycle or take horse and buggy rides to explore the peaceful state park. Unusual rock formations have bewitching names such as Devil's Kitchen and Skull Cave. Arch Rock is a smooth, fifty-foot-wide limestone arch. Native Americans believe the arch is a door through which spirits enter the island.

Mackinac Island is rich in history. The beautifully preserved Grand Hotel and the many Victorian cottages make it look as though time has stood still. At Fort Mackinac, costumed soldiers salute with muskets and cannons. One eighteenth-century soldier wrote, "the air up here is so healthy you have to go somewhere else to die."

The limestone Arch Rock on Mackinac Island is 150 feet high and has a span of 50 feet.

The Upper Peninsula displays nature at its best. Scattered towns have only a few thousand people each. Visitors can eat local treats, like Marquette's famous Cornish pasties.

One of the most scenic stretches is along Pictured Rocks National Lakeshore. Pictured Rocks was the nation's first national lakeshore. Towering cliffs and pine forests frame 42 miles of white sand beaches on southern Lake Superior. The sandstone cliffs soar 200 feet above the lake and are etched by the water and wind into a variety of shapes and colors. The Ojibwe called the cliffs Pictured Rocks for their awesome colors. Today, visitors can tour the shores, a reconstructed logging camp, and an iron-smelting town.

In October 2006, Picture Rocks National Lakeshore celebrated its fortieth anniversary as America's first national lakeshore.

SOO LOCKS BOAT TOURS
GEORGE A. STINSON
Soo Locks operate the world's largest waterway traffic system in the world.

Each winter, the peninsula turns into a wonderland of outdoor sports. In February Houghton hosts a winter carnival, which features the Snow Competition. Mackinaw's Mush Annual Dog Sled Race happens the same month. By then, athletes need to warm up in the National Ski Hall of Fame in Ishpeming, where the nation pays tribute to skiing greats.

Sault Sainte Marie, Michigan's oldest city, is unlike any other town. The city of 15,000 people is famous for the Soo Locks. The Soo is the busiest and largest link system between Lakes Huron and Superior. Boat tours carry visitors through the locks, sometimes alongside ocean-going freighters. The nearby park has a lock overlook and a view of the museum ship *Valley Camp*.

The Locks Park Walkway takes hikers on a tour of the town's historic waterfront. Baraga House, the 1864 home of Bishop Frederick Baraga, stands on the trail. Baraga was the Upper Peninsula's first Roman Catholic bishop, but he was best known as the Snowshoe Priest for the way he traveled in snow.

Michigan has many more exciting places to visit. "With 250,000 acres, we have the largest park system in the Midwest," Ron Nagel of the Michigan parks department declares. "Twenty-five million people visit each year." And more keep coming. Michigan is a state that casts a spell over visitors, beckoning people back for more.

E PLURIBUS UNUM
TUEBOR
SI QUÆRIS PENINSULAM AMŒNAM
CIRCUMSPICE

THE FLAG: The Michigan state flag has the state seal on a field of blue.

THE GREAT SEAL OF THE STATE OF MICHIGAN
A. D. MDCCCXXXV.
E PLURIBUS UNUM
TUEBOR
SI QUÆRIS PENINSULAM AMŒNAM
CIRCUMSPICE

THE SEAL: The state seal has a shield at the center that displays the sun rising over a lake. A man on the shore has his right hand raised to symbolize peace. In his left hand is a rifle, showing a readiness to defend state and country. To the sides of the shield are an elk and a moose, and above the shield is a bald eagle. The shield also has three Latin phrases, Tuebor, *or "I will defend";* E pluribus unum, *or "From many, one"; and* Si Quaeris Peninsulam Amoenam Circumpice, *or "The Great Seal of the State of Michigan."*

State Survey

Statehood: January 26, 1837

Origin of Name: Michigan takes its name from Lake Michigan. *Michigan* comes from the Ojibwe word *michigama*, which means "great water."

Nicknames: Wolverine State, or The Great Lake State

Capital: Lansing

Motto: If You Seek a Pleasant Peninsula, Look About You

Robin

Bird: Robin

Fish: Brook trout

Reptile: Painted turtle

Flower: Apple blossom

Tree: White pine

Stone: Petoskey stone

Gem: Isle Royale greenstone

Soil: Kalkaska sand

Apple blossoms

MICHIGAN, MY MICHIGAN

Unofficial State Song

This song was composed in 1911 and has been sung as the unofficial state song for many years. It has never been adopted as the official song because each time the state legislature has considered it, other songs have been proposed as well.

Douglas Malloch **W. Otto Meissner**

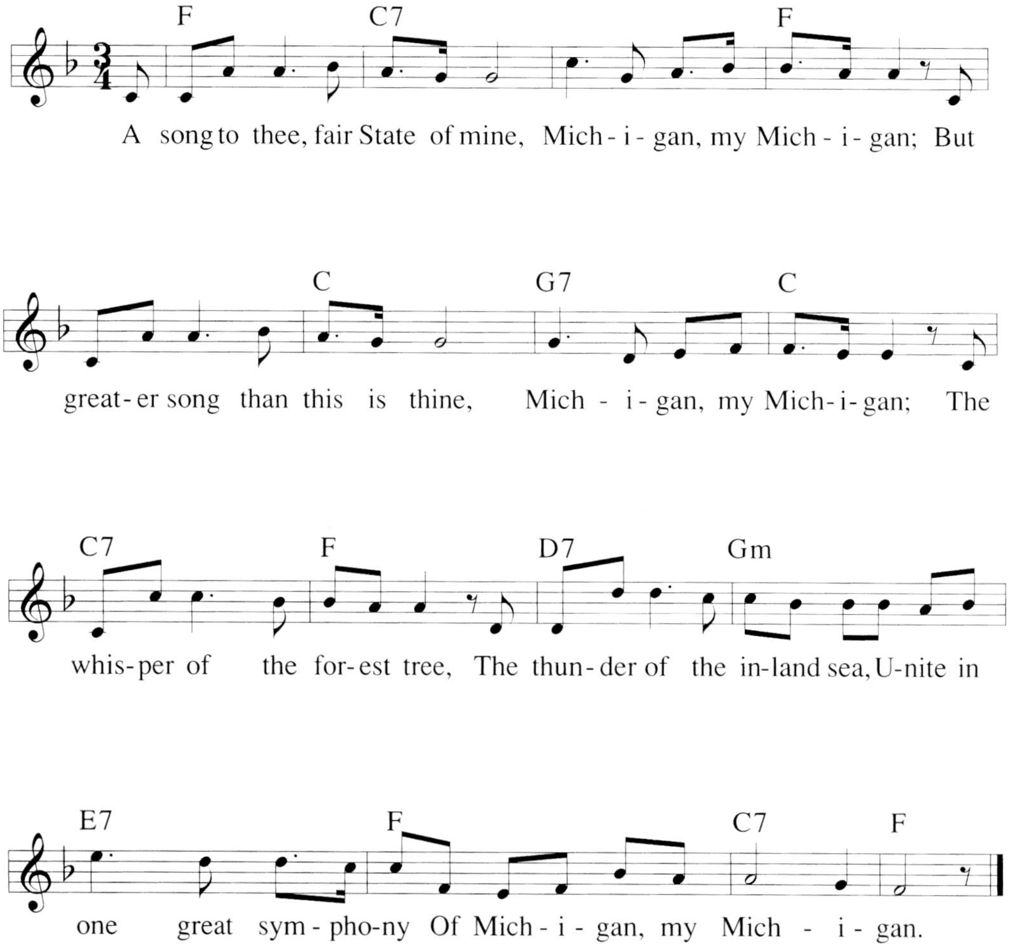
F C7 F
A song to thee, fair State of mine, Mich - i - gan, my Mich - i - gan; But
C G7 C
great- er song than this is thine, Mich - i - gan, my Mich- i- gan; The
C7 F D7 Gm
whis- per of the for- est tree, The thun- der of the in-land sea, U-nite in
E7 F C7 F
one great sym - pho-ny Of Mich - i - gan, my Mich - i - gan.

GEOGRAPHY

Highest Point: 1,979 feet above sea level, at Mount Arvon

Lowest Point: 572 feet above sea level, along the coast of Lake Erie

Area: 58,527 square miles

Greatest Distance North to South: 490 miles

Greatest Distance East to West: 240 miles

Bordering States: Upper Peninsula: Wisconsin to the west; Lower Peninsula: Ohio and Indiana to the south

Hottest Recorded Temperature: 112 degrees Fahrenheit at Mio on July 13, 1936

Coldest Recorded Temperature: –51 degrees Fahrenheit at Vanderbilt on February 9, 1934

Average Annual Precipitation: 32 inches

Major Rivers: Au Sable, Cass, Clinton, Detroit, Escanaba, Grand, Huron, Kalamazoo, Manistee, Manistique, Menominee, Muskegon, Ontonagan, Pere Marquette, Raisin, Saginaw, Saint Clair, Saint Joseph, Sturgeon, Tahquamenon, Whitefish

Major Lakes: Black, Burt, Charlevoix, Crystal, Fletcher Pond, Gogebic, Grand, Higgins, Houghton, Hubbard, Indian, Manistique, Mullet, Torch

Trees: aspen, beech, birch, cedar, elm, fir, hemlock, hickory, maple, oak, pine, spruce

Wild Plants: aster, bittersweet, blackberry, blueberry, chicory, clematis, cranberry, currant, daisy, elderberry, fern, goldenrod, gooseberry, grape, iris, lady's slipper, mandrake, orange milkweed, raspberry, rose, sunflower, tiger lily, trillium, violet

Animals: badger, beaver, black bear, bobcat, elk, fox, moose, opossum, otter, porcupine, rabbit, raccoon, skunk, squirrel, timber wolf, white-tailed deer

White-tailed deer fawn

Birds: bald eagle, bluebird, blue jay, cardinal, duck, goose, horned owl, hummingbird, mourning dove, osprey, partridge, pheasant, pileated woodpecker, quail, robin, ruffed grouse, snipe, swift, wild turkey, woodcock

Fish: bass, bluegill, carp, catfish, crappie, lake herring, lake trout, muskellunge, perch, pike, salmon, smelt, sturgeon, trout, walleye, whitefish

Endangered Animals: American burying beetle, barn owl, bigeye chub, catspaw mussel, copperbelly water snake, cougar, gray wolf, Hungerford's crawling water beetle, Indiana bat, ironcolor shiner, Kirtland's snake, Kirtland's warbler, loggerhead shrike, lynx, Mitchell's satyr butterfly, northern madtom, peregrine falcon, phlox moth, piping plover, river darter, salamander mussel, short-eared owl, small-mouth salamander

Gray wolf

Endangered Plants: American hart's-tongue fern, dwarf lake iris, eastern prairie fringed orchid, Houghton's goldenrod, Michigan monkey-flower, Pitcher's thistle, western prairie fringed orchid

TIMELINE

Michigan History

1600s The Ottawa, Ojibwe, and Potawatomi live in Michigan.

1620 French explorer Etienne Brulé is the first European known to reach Michigan when he lands near present-day Sault Saint Marie.

1634 Jean Nicolet of France explores the Great Lakes region.

1668 The first permanent European settlement is founded in Michigan at Sault Saint Marie by French priest Jacques Marquette.

1671 The French build Fort Michilimackinac on the southern shore of the Straits of Mackinac.

1701 Antoine de la Mothe Cadillac builds a French fort at the site of present-day Detroit.

1760 The French and Indian War ends; the winning British take over most French lands in North America.

1775 American Revolution begins.

1783 British forces remain in the forts at Detroit and Mackinac even though Great Britain has lost the American Revolution.

1787 Michigan becomes part of the Northwest Territory, which is eventually divided into five states.

1796 American troops occupy the forts at Detroit and Mackinac.

1805 The Michigan Territory is created; fire destroys most of Detroit.

1812 The War of 1812 begins; General William Hull surrenders the American fort at Detroit to the British without firing a shot.

1813 Detroit is recaptured by the Americans.

1837 Michigan becomes the twenty-sixth state.

1847 Michigan's capital is moved from Detroit to Lansing.

1855 The locks at Sault Saint Marie are completed, allowing ships to travel more easily between Lakes Huron and Superior.

1861–1865 About 90,000 Michiganders serve in the Union Army during the Civil War.

1897 The Olds Motor Works becomes the first automobile manufacturer in Michigan.

1898 The Kellogg brothers make the first wheat flakes.

1903 The Ford Motor Company is created.

1925 Oil is discovered in the Saginaw area.

1941–1945 Around 673,000 Michiganders serve in the U.S. armed forces during World War II.

1942 Automobile makers switch from manufacturing cars and trucks for the general public to making war materials.

1963 Martin Luther King Jr. leads 125,000 people in a civil rights march in Detroit.

1967 During riots in Detroit, forty-three people die and more than 1,300 buildings are burned.

1973 Coleman Young is elected Detroit's first African-American mayor.

1974 Gerald Ford of Grand Rapids becomes president of the United States when Richard Nixon resigns.

1976 Michiganders vote to ban throwaway beverage containers; all bottles and cans must be returned for deposit and recycling.

1993 Julie Krone of Eau Claire becomes the first woman jockey to win major racing events.

2002 Michiganders elect Jennifer Granholm as their first female and forty-seventh governor; Detroit Red Wings win their tenth Stanley Cup.

2004 Detroit Pistons win their third NBA championship.

2006 Detroit hosts the National Football League's Super Bowl.

ECONOMY

Agricultural Products: apples, asparagus, beans, blueberries, cattle, cherries, chickens, corn, cucumbers, dairy products, hay, hogs, mink, oats, peaches, pears, potatoes, soybeans, strawberries, sugar beets, wheat

Manufactured Products: automobiles, automobile parts, buses, chemicals, fabricated metal items, iron, machine parts and tools, medical supplies, office furniture, processed foods, sports equipment, trucks, wood products

60338

Automobiles

Natural Resources: copper, gypsum, iron ore, limestone, natural gas, oil, salt, sand and gravel, shale, timber

Business and Trade: communications, finance, insurance, real estate, transportation, wholesale and retail trade

CALENDAR OF CELEBRATIONS

Ice Sculpture Spectacular Plymouth is home to this icy festival, the oldest and largest ice-carving event in the United States. Every January, hundreds of thousands of visitors gather to watch two hundred contestants transform blocks of ice into beautiful sculptures.

Ice Sculpture Spectacular

North American Snowmobile Festival Participants find lots of fast winter fun when ten thousand snowmobiles take to the ice on Lake Cadillac in January or February. This festival features snowmobile races as well as snow sculpting and sleigh rides.

Irish Festival Visitors like to wear green at this celebration of everything Irish. At the March festival in Clare, you can march in a parade with a leprechaun band, enter a silly bed race, and dance a jig to Irish music.

Maple Syrup Festival At this Vermontville festival held every April, you can see how syrup is made and eat maple fudge, maple cream, and caramel corn covered in maple syrup. There's also a children's parade and a petting zoo.

National Morel Mushroom-Hunting Festival Tasty but hard to find morel mushrooms are the focus of this May festival in Boyne City. Visitors can take part in the official mushroom-hunt competition or just eat special dishes made with morels. Children can listen to a nature talk and take part in a mini-hunt for candy and prizes.

Highland Festival and Games This Scottish festival held in Alma each May features games of strength and skill, such as tossing the caber—a 20-foot-long section of telephone pole. There's also bagpipe music and Scottish meat pies.

Tulip Time Six million tulips are in bloom during this May festival in the town of Holland. Visitors can also view Dutch dancing, street scrubbing, and wooden-shoe making.

National Cherry Festival Traverse City, "Cherry Capital of the World," hosts this festival in July. There are parades, fireworks, concerts, an air show, and, of course, a cherry pie-eating contest.

Au Sable River International Canoe Marathon and Au Sable River Festival An all-night canoe race on the Au Sable River between the towns of Grayling and Oscoda is the highlight of this July festival. Along the 120-mile route, visitors cheer on the paddlers. In the towns, there are parades, arts and crafts, and ice cream and other foods.

Nautical City Festival Rogers City is the home of this celebration of life on the shores of Lake Huron. Visitors can watch a parade, have fun at a carnival, or take part in a beach volleyball competition. There's also a fish fry at this late July-early August festival.

Michigan Festival This ten-day festival in East Lansing every August celebrates all the best of Michigan, from folklife to Native American dancing. Visitors can bring blankets for nighttime outdoor concerts with nationally known acts. A special children's festival features magic shows, music, and dancing.

Mackinac Bridge Walk Michiganders have only one chance a year to walk across the 5-mile bridge that connects Michigan's Upper and Lower peninsulas. Thousands of walkers, including the governor of Michigan, show up for this Labor Day event in Mackinaw City and Saint Ignace.

Mackinac Bridge Walk

Red Flannel Festival During the end of September, the town of Cedar Springs begins its celebration of these red, one-piece undergarments. At the festival, visitors will find a carnival, crafts fair, tractor pull, music, and great food. Vistors can even buy a specially made red flannel union suit.

Color Cruise and Island Festival A trip on a paddle-wheel riverboat on the Grand River is the perfect way to view fall colors during this October festival. On Second Island near the town of Grand Ledge, visitors can see old-fashioned blacksmithing and wool-spinning and sample bean soup cooked in an old black kettle.

International Festival of Lights Millions of lights brighten the town of Battle Creek during this festival in November and December. Exhibits include Trees Around the World and a giant, glowing Tony the Tiger.

Victorian Sleighbell Parade and Old Christmas Weekend The town of Manistee celebrates an old-fashioned Christmas every December with historically decorated buildings. Visitors can munch on roasted chestnuts while watching the parade, which features horse-drawn wagons and characters in period costumes.

STATE STARS

Ralph Bunche (1904–1971), of Detroit, helped found the United Nations (UN) and then served as UN undersecretary from 1955 to 1971. In 1950, Bunche was the first African American to win the Nobel Peace Prize. He received the honor for helping to negotiate peace in the Middle East.

Bruce Catton (1899–1978), born in Petoskey, was a Pulitzer Prize-winning author. Catton won the prize in 1953 for *A Stillness at Appomattox*, one of the many books he wrote about the Civil War.

Madonna

Madonna Louise Veronica Ciccone (1958–), the superstar better known simply as Madonna, was born in Bay City. Her videos and concerts made her a superstar, and her ever-changing style has had an influence on fashion worldwide. She has had many hit singles, including "Material Girl" and "Vogue." She has also acted in movies such as *Dick Tracy*, *A League of Their Own*, and *Evita*, and has written several children's books.

Tyrus "Ty" Cobb (1886–1961) played baseball with the Detroit Tigers for twenty-two years and managed the team for six more. Considered one of the game's greats, Cobb had more than four thousand hits, won twelve batting titles, and was elected to the Baseball Hall of Fame in 1936.

Francis Ford Coppola (1939–), of Detroit, gained fame as a movie writer, producer, and director. Coppola has won five Academy Awards. His movies include *The Godfather*, *The Godfather Part II*, and *Apocalypse Now*.

George Armstrong Custer (1839–1876), although Ohio-born, grew up in Monroe. Custer first earned fame as a brave young general in the Civil War. He was later killed at the Battle of the Little Bighorn while waging a ruthless war against the Native Americans in the West.

Gerald R. Ford (1913–   ) grew up in Grand Rapids and attended the University of Michigan. Ford became a U.S. representative from Michigan and was chosen to be vice president when Spiro Agnew resigned that post in 1973. In 1974, Ford became the thirty-eighth president when Richard Nixon resigned.

Henry Ford (1863–1947), of Dearborn, built his first car in 1896 and founded the Ford Motor Company in 1903. Ford sold thousands of his Model T, one of the first cars that was affordable to most Americans.

Daniel Gerber (1898–1974) saw how difficult it was for his wife to make food for their baby and decided to make feeding time easier for mothers everywhere. He began canning baby food in his food factory in Fremont in 1927. Within twenty years, Gerber's company was selling millions of jars of baby food every day.

Berry Gordy Jr. (1929–   ), a Detroit native, founded Motown Records. Beginning in 1959, Gordy's company signed a number of African-American acts, including the Supremes, Smokey Robinson and the Miracles, and Stevie Wonder and turned them into major stars.

Earvin "Magic" Johnson (1959–), of Lansing, is recognized as one of basketball's greatest players. After helping his team at Michigan State University win the national championship in 1979, he led the Los Angeles Lakers to five NBA titles in the 1980s. Johnson retired from basketball in 1991 after announcing that he was infected with the AIDS virus. He now works to educate people about the disease. He wrote a book for young people called *What You Can Do to Avoid AIDS.*

John Harvey (1852–1943) and **William Keith** (1860-1951) **Kellogg** were brothers from Battle Creek who discovered how to make corn flakes. John was the inventor, but William began the Battle Creek Toasted Corn Flake Company in 1906, which became known as the Kellogg Company.

Julie Krone (1963–), Benton Harbor born and Eau Claire raised, became the only female jockey to win the Triple Crown and Belmont Stakes. She continued to pile up three thousand wins, the most of any woman. Krone retired in 1999 but reappeared in 2002 to win the 2003 Breeders' Cup race.

Charles Lindbergh (1902–1974), the first person to fly across the Atlantic Ocean alone, was born in Detroit. Lindbergh made his daring 33.5-hour flight in 1927 and instantly became a celebrity around the world.

Charles Lindbergh

Joe Louis (1914–1981) took up boxing after he moved to Detroit as a young boy. The "Brown Bomber," as he was called, became a professional boxer in 1934. He held the heavyweight boxing championship for almost twelve years—longer than any other fighter.

Malcolm X (1915–1965), an important African-American leader of the 1960s, grew up in Lansing. Born Malcolm Little, he became a Black Muslim and changed his last name to X to represent the unknown African name of his ancestors. Malcolm X urged African Americans to be proud of their black heritage and to work for equal rights. He was assassinated after breaking with the Black Muslims and changing his views on how blacks should achieve equality.

Malcolm X

Joyce Carol Oates (1938–) is an award-winning author who taught English at the University of Detroit. Oates has often used Detroit as the setting for her stories. Her novels include *Them* and *Wonderland.*

Ransom Eli Olds (1864–1950) of Lansing played an important role in the beginning of Michigan's automobile industry. In 1897 he started the Olds Motor Works, the first automobile factory in Michigan. Two years later, he began calling his cars "Oldsmobiles."

Patricia Polacco (1944–), award-winning children's book author and illustrator, was Lansing-born and Williamston- and Union City-raised. Among the children's books she has written are *Emma Kate*, *Pink and Say*, and *Thunder Cake*.

Walter Reuther (1907–1970) helped create better working conditions for autoworkers in Michigan and throughout the United States. After moving to Detroit in 1926, Reuther worked to organize the United Auto Workers. He served as president of the union from 1946 until 1970.

"Sugar" Ray Robinson (1921–1989), of Detroit, won boxing championships in both the welterweight and middleweight classes. Often called the best fighter, pound-for-pound, in the history of boxing, Robinson won 174 matches with 109 knockouts, a boxing record.

Diana Ross (1944–) was one of the biggest stars to come out of Motown Records. Singing with the Supremes, she had many hit songs, including "Where Did Our Love Go?" Born in Detroit, Ross went on to a solo singing career and starring roles in films such as *Lady Sings the Blues* and *The Wiz*.

Steven Seagal (1951–) has kicked and punched his way through a number of action movies. A martial arts expert, Seagal has starred in films such as *Above the Law* and *Under Siege*. Seagal was born in Lansing.

Lily Tomlin (1939–   ) is a talented performer who has worked on television, in movies, and on the stage. Born in Detroit, Tomlin began her career as a comedian in the 1960s and won a Grammy in 1971 for a comedy album. She has starred in several motion pictures, including *Nashville* and *Nine to Five*, as well as in Broadway shows.

Lily Tomlin

Chris Van Allsburg (1949–   ), a writer and illustrator of children's books, is from Grand Rapids. He won Caldecott Awards for his drawings in *The Polar Express* and *Jumanji*.

Thomas H. Weller (1915–   ) is a Nobel Prize-winning scientist from Ann Arbor. Weller won the Nobel Prize in 1954 for his work with the poliovirus. He is also well known for his research with other diseases, including rubella and chicken pox.

Stevie Wonder (1950–   ), who has been making records since he was thirteen, was born in Saginaw. Blind since birth, Wonder writes, sings, and plays his own music. His hit songs have included "Living for the City" and "I Just Called to Say I Love You."

Coleman Young (1918–   ) was Detroit's first African-American mayor. Serving from 1974 to 1994, Young led Detroit longer than any other mayor.

TOUR THE STATE

Henry Ford Museum and Greenfield Village (Dearborn) Some of the best of American history is found at this well-known attraction. The museum covers all aspects of American life, and the collections include items such as the chair in which Abraham Lincoln was sitting when he was assassinated. Greenfield Village contains many important buildings from America's past. There is the home of Henry Ford, the tavern where Lincoln practiced law, and the laboratory of inventor Thomas Edison.

Museum of African American History (Detroit) This new museum houses the country's largest collection of memorabilia relating to black history. Exhibits cover African-American history from the slave trade to the present. Visitors can even walk through a replica of a slave ship.

The Detroit Institute of Arts (Detroit) Art from around the world is featured at this well-respected museum, which displays everything from medieval knights' armor to African- and Native-American art.

Motown Historical Museum (Detroit) The great sounds of Motown are remembered in this old brick house where the company started in the early 1960s. The museum contains the original recording studio as well as musical instruments and other items that belonged to the Motown stars.

Detroit Zoological Park (Royal Oak) One of the largest zoos in the country, this park features animals in cageless, natural settings. Visitors can see such favorites as chimpanzees, penguins, and polar bears.

Lionel Trains Visitor Center (Chesterfield) The Lionel Company's Visitor Center is a delight for model-train lovers. The main exhibit features ten trains running on 1,000 feet of track. A number of other operating train models are also on display.

Michigan Space and Science Center (Jackson) Space suits, satellites, the Apollo 9 capsule, a model of the Hubble Space Telescope, and a moon rock are only a few of the things to see at this out-of-this-world attraction. Visitors can also climb inside a space capsule and view an 85-foot-tall rocket.

State Capitol (Lansing) Built in 1879, the Michigan State Capitol was one of the first state capitols to be patterned after the U.S. Capitol in Washington, D.C. A tour of the building's beautiful interior reveals Civil War battle flags, portraits of Michigan governors, and other items from Michigan history.

Cikibuak Michilimackinac (Mackinaw City) Several buildings, including a guardhouse, barracks, blacksmith's shop, church, and trader's house, have been reconstructed at this site of a French fort. Costumed actors dressed as British soldiers, French fur traders, and Native Americans help bring history to life.

Fort Mackinac (Mackinac Island) This restored British and American fort features costumed guides playing military music and firing muskets and cannons. There is also a Children's Discovery Room with hands-on exhibits and period costumes for kids to try on.

Marquette Mission Park and Museum of Ojibwa Culture (Saint Ignace) A statue of Father Jacques Marquette and a display on his life can be found at this site that is thought to be Marquette's burial place. The accompanying museum displays many artifacts related to Ojibwe Indian life.

Tahquamenon Falls State Park (Paradise) Upper Tahquamenon Falls, measuring 200 feet across with a drop of 50 feet, is the second-largest waterfall east of the Mississippi River. The lower falls are a series of drops and rapids in the Tahquamenon River. Both sets of falls are easily reached along the park's many miles of hiking trails.

Shipwreck Historical Museum (Whitefish Point) Visitors here can learn the stories of some of Lake Superior's 550 shipwrecks. Photos and artifacts present the history of the lake's most famous shipwrecks, including the *Edmund Fitzgerald*. The neighboring 148-year-old lighthouse is also open to visitors.

Pictured Rocks National Lakeshore (Munising) The Pictured Rocks of this park are spectacular wind- and water-carved cliffs rising 200 feet above the surface of Lake Superior. Summer activities include swimming, hiking, and scenic boat rides to view the Pictured Rocks. In the winter, plenty of snow makes for great cross-country skiing and snowmobiling.

Michigan Iron Industry Museum (Negaunee) Visitors here learn about the early history of Michigan's iron-mining industry. Exhibits include an 1860s locomotive that was used to haul iron ore.

Spirit of the Woods Museum (Elk Rapids) Michigan's Native Americans and native animals are featured in this museum. Native American items such as arrowheads, bows, and moccasins, are on display, along with preserved specimens of North American animals, including wolves, bears, bison, deer, and beavers.

Sleeping Bear Dunes National Lakeshore (Empire) Although this park also offers swimming, fishing, hiking, and bird-watching, the favorite activity here is dune climbing. Awesome dunes, some over 400 feet high, make for adventurous, and difficult, climbing. The park's observation platforms offer terrific views of Lake Michigan.

Gerald R. Ford Museum (Grand Rapids) Dedicated to the only American president not elected by the people, this museum includes a replica of the White House's Oval Office as it looked when Ford was in office. There are also exhibits on events from that period, such as Richard Nixon's fall from the presidency and America's Bicentennial.

Kalamazoo Aviation History Museum (Kalamazoo) Great American airplanes are the focus of this museum. Warplanes and other aircraft from American history are on display, and during the summer some even perform flying demonstrations. An activity room includes a flight simulator for visitors to try.

FUN FACTS

If you're wondering which way the wind is blowing, it's easy to find out in Montague. The town has the world's largest weather vane. The weather vane stands 48 feet tall and weighs 3,500 pounds.

It has a 26-foot-long wind arrow and is decorated with a 14-foot-long replica of a Great Lakes sailing ship.

Michigan offers a special program for drivers who have a fear of crossing long bridges. At the Mackinac Bridge, which is 200 feet high and 5 miles long, timid drivers can let a state employee drive their car across the bridge while they sit back and close their eyes.

The record for spitting a cherry pit is 72 feet, 7.5 inches, which was set at the International Cherry Pit Spitting Championship in Eau Claire in 1988. Contestants from around the world gather for a chance to win the yearly competition.

A lot of Michigan beaches are pretty to walk along; some will even sing to you. The beaches at Grand Haven are one of the few places where singing sand can be found. The tiny sand particles make a whistling sound as you walk.

Scientists think they may have found the world's largest living organism beneath the Michigan-Wisconsin border. A single fungus—a large mushroom—that covers 37 acres and weighs 1,000 tons is growing beneath the surface of the ground there. The organism may be 1,500 years old, and scientists are not sure whether they have found all of it.

Find Out More

If you'd like to find out more about Michigan, look in your school library, local library, bookstore, or video store. You can also surf the Internet. Here are some resources to help you begin your search.

MICHIGAN PEOPLE AND SPECIAL INTEREST BOOKS

Aronson, Virginia. *The History of Motown*. New York: Chelsea House, 2001.

Barker, Charles Ferguson. *Under Michigan: The Story of Michigan's Rocks and Fossils*. Detroit: Wayne State University Press, 2005.

Kammerad, Kevin. *A Curious Glimpse of Michigan*. Auburn Hills, MI: EDCO Publishing, 2004.

Lytle, Robert. *A Pitch in Time*. Auburn Hills, MI: EDCO Publishing, 2002.

McCarthy, Pat. *Henry Ford: Building Cars for Everyone*. Berkeley Heights, NJ: Enslow Publishers, 2002.

Rinaldi, Ann. *Girl in Blue*. New York: Scholastic, 2001.

WEB SITES

Settling a State: The Boy Governor

www.sos.state.mi.us/history/museum/explore/museums/hismus/prehist/settling/boygov.html.

Visit this site to read the story of Michigan's first and youngest governor at age nineteen.

The Barn Exhibit

www.sos.state.mi.us/history/museum/musewalk/barn

Take a tour of the Walker Tavern, barns, and road in the nineteenth century.

Kid's Stuff from the Michigan Historical Museum

www.michigan.gov/mikids

Go here for activities, stories, poems, and historic documents for kids.

Michigan's State Symbols

www.michigan.gov/documents/mhc_mhm_statesymbols2002_47909

This brochure written for kids explains which are Michigan's state symbols.

The Mitten: Michigan History Magazine for Kids

www.michiganhistorymagazine.com/kids

Check out regular kids' online magazines, each about a topic important in Michigan history.

Michigan Department of Natural Resources L.A.P.'s

www.dnr.state.mi.us/edu/DNRIntroPages/DNRlaps

Learn more about this millennium education project that offers information and activities about preserving Michigan's outdoor heritage.

Index

Page numbers in **boldface** are illustrations and charts.

ABOUT THE AUTHOR

Marlene Targ Brill writes about many different topics, from history, biographies, and health care to world peace and tooth fairies. Her favorite books help readers learn new and interesting facts, whether through fiction or nonfiction. As a teacher, Brill shared fun facts with students who had special needs. Now she tells stories to all children and adults in her more than sixty books. To find facts for Celebrate the States, Second Edition, *Michigan,* Brill toured the state and met people who lived and worked throughout the state's cities and towns. She visited old friends from when she lived in Michigan. After traveling Michigan's nooks and crannies, she went home to Illinois to write about what she learned.